ON A WING
and a Prayer

ROYAN YULE

ON A WING *and a Prayer*

First published in Great Britain in 2012 by The Derby Books Publishing Company Limited, 3 The Parker Centre, Derby, DE21 4SZ.

ISBN 978-1-78091-049-9
Printed and bound by CPI Antony Rowe, Chippenham.

CONTENTS

Acknowledgements 7
Introduction 9

1. Retrospect 11
2. Early Years 16
3. I Join the RAF 22
4. North America Bound 32
5. Home on the *Queen Mary* 41
6. Crewing Up 46
7. Wickenby 55
8. The Crew's First Operation 63
9. Operation Hurricane 73
10. On a Wing and a Prayer 80
11. The King's Commission 88
12. Royan 98
13. The Beginning of Fear 108
14. Dresden 120
15. 'I am English' 130
16. Farewell to Roger 2 138
17. Hitler's Oil 144
18. Tour's End 157
19. Post-war Years 164
20. A Voice From the Past 175
21. Epilogue 184

Bibliography 188
Index 189

ACKNOWLEDGEMENTS

For the most part, this book is made up of the recollections of my own experiences both during my time with Bomber Command and otherwise. However, when we were on operations we often had very limited information on the outcome of raids or what may have happened to other crews for example. I also didn't know the truth about certain matters, such as certain aspects of the German fighter tactics until after the war, although I undoubtedly witnessed the devastating results of these. Accordingly, over the years, I have carried out a fair amount of research to gather background information and in this respect I am particularly indebted to firstly, Martin Middlebrook and Chris Everitt for *The Bomber Command War Diaries* (Midland Publishing) and also to Jonathan Falconer for his *Bomber Command Handbook* (Sutton Publishing).

I have also gathered a great deal of information from 12 & 626 Squadrons' operational records and a special thanks goes here to Tim Brett and Anne Law of the Wickenby Memorial Collection for information on operations flown from Wickenby and the crews who took part. Tim and Anne were also extremely hospitable to my son when he visited Wickenby airfield in the summer of 2011, following which they did me the honour of making up an individual folder of my operational record for the museum.

With regard to the passage on Gordon Cummins, 'The Blackout Ripper', I referred for information on his crimes to an article entitled 'Blackout Killers' in Vol. 5, Issue 72 of *Murder Casebook* (Marshall Cavendish).

In relation to my post-war flying career I am indebted to the late Roddy Robertson MBE for *The Story of 612 (County of Aberdeen) Squadron* (1989). Roddy was a pal from the early days of the post-war squadron and was to become its last Squadron Commander. Another good pal and 612 pilot, Johnny Milne, was instrumental in having Roddy's work published.

Special thanks also to my publishers, DB Publishing, for showing faith in this project from the outset and for their unfailing support and endeavours in bringing it to fruition.

Last but not least, I would like to acknowledge the contribution made by my son, also called Royan, without whose help and perseverance this book would simply not have been accomplished.

INTRODUCTION

For many years after the war I had no real inclination to write down my memoirs. For one thing I was too busy getting on with my life and, furthermore, I felt that there were thousands of others who had gone through a similar experience and therefore there was nothing unique about me or my crew. It was only following an unexpected reunion with my former regular crew members at Wickenby in 1982 that I resolved to write an account of my experiences during my time with Bomber Command while my memory of events was still relatively fresh. I never intended for this to be published in book form and it was done really for the benefit of any family members or friends who might be interested in reading it. I also submitted the odd article to the *Wickenby Register* over the years which they kindly included in their issues.

More recently, however, I have allowed myself to be persuaded by my son that there might be a story worth telling and as he diplomatically puts it, there are not many of us who are still around to tell it! To this end he has encouraged me to extend the manuscript into a fuller biography which also covers my earlier life and post-war career.

Everything that I have written in this book is true to the best of my knowledge and recollection and there is nothing which has been invented or over-dramatised. The only qualification to this is that in three instances I have changed the names of individuals about whom I write in terms which are less than complimentary. Although the men in question are almost certainly no longer alive (at least two of them were quite a bit older than me), I would not wish to risk causing possible embarrassment to their families when they themselves are no longer in a position to respond. Having said this, I stand by my remarks and have included the references to these men because I consider my experiences in relation to them to be integral to my story. I do express certain opinions in this book about the leadership of Bomber Command and about the bombing campaign in general and the Dresden raid in particular, which I appreciate not everyone may agree with. I would just say on this, that I have yet to find a former member of Bomber Command who would fundamentally disagree with the general gist of my comments on these issues. I also recognise that I may quite possibly have unwittingly included the odd inaccuracy in this account. If that proves to be the case then I alone take full responsibility and would welcome hearing from any reader who would care to draw my attention to any alleged errors or discrepancies.

Sadly, of my fellow crew members, only Greg Mayes in Australia is still alive. However, I hope that the crew members' families and indeed anyone who knew them will take justified pride from reading my account and seeing how much I valued and respected them all.

Chapter 1
RETROSPECT

Friday 12 July 1940 was a bright sunny day in Aberdeen. From the back steps of my home in Jasmine Terrace I watched an unequal battle between three Spitfires and a solitary Heinkel III bomber. The Heinkel had just dropped a stick of bombs in a line from the University sports ground at Kings College to Urquhart Road, which is close to Jasmine Terrace, and finally to York Street, near the shipbuilding yards of Hall Russell and Alexander Hall & Co. At that time I was an apprentice engineer with A. Hall & Co. and I was to see the devastation at first hand when, shortly afterwards, I cycled down to work following my lunch break. In the meantime, however, the Spitfires took it in turn to attack the bomber which, riddled with bullets, eventually crashed on the site of a new ice rink being built at South Anderson Drive, near the old Bridge of Dee.

I had to pass by where the bombs had exploded in York Street to get to my place of work and the carnage that I witnessed is emblazoned in my memory. I had to lift my bicycle on to my shoulder to step over girders and debris that cluttered the road. Then I almost stepped on what looked like the carcass of a dog shorn of its skin, until I realised that it was the trunk of a human body, minus limbs, head and skin. I carried on past the huge doors of the boiler shop at Hall Russell where a dead horse lay partly over another corpse, who I took to be the driver of the cart. His clothes had been blown off and the slashes on the skin were coated with congealed blood. My nostrils were assailed with a sickly smell which I assumed was from the cordite in the bombs. Passing a broken gas lamp post, which was shooting a jet of flame 6ft vertically into the air, I came upon a pile of rubble against the wall opposite the dead horse and driver. A wrecked bicycle lay to one side and, protruding from the rubble, was a pair of hands. It later transpired that these human remains were those of a very popular student from Aberdeen University who was doing his six months practical engineering experience with us.

Further on, at the intersection of York Place and York Street, the front of the Neptune Bar had been blown wide open and dead bodies were lying around inside. Flames were roaring from the stump of another street gas lamp on the corner.

The sun was shining and all was silent apart from the roaring gas lamps. I must have arrived on the scene about 10–15 minutes after the bombs had dropped and I don't recall there being any sign of the emergency services at that point. Death was all around but I do not personally remember seeing anyone lying obviously injured or hearing any cries for help. I just carried on to my own place of work at A. Hall & Co.'s workshop which had not been hit.

I was experiencing war from the non-combatant side but, perhaps strangely, I did not feel hatred towards the German aircrew responsible for this raid. I found out later that all four of the Heinkel's crew had perished, but the way I saw it, they had died carrying out an extremely dangerous raid on a legitimate industrial target. They might have got away with it but for the fact that the 'City of Edinburgh' 603 Spitfire Squadron was stationed at nearby Dyce Airfield at that time. I heard or read later that the German pilot was the holder of the Iron Cross. The ice rink was never completed and houses were built where the original rink was planned. Thirty-two people were killed and eighty more injured during this raid.

That air battle probably gave me the yearning to join the RAF as aircrew. However, at that time it was not possible for me to join the RAF because I was in a reserved occupation. That was all to change the following year, in 1941, when it was decreed that men in reserved occupations could volunteer for RAF aircrew but only as pilot or observer. Little could I foresee, therefore, on that terrible summer's day, that in four years' time I would be piloting a Lancaster bomber over enemy territory, one very small cog in the machine tasked with, to paraphrase Sir Winston Churchill, ensuring that Germany reaped the whirlwind for sowing the wind of the blitz on British cities.

* * * * *

At the time of the Hall Russell raid I was 18 years old and not long into the third year of what was scheduled to be a five year apprenticeship. By then I had quite a responsible job on the surface table at A. Hall & Co. which involved obtaining drawings of engines etc. and transferring the dimensions on to castings and forgings which then had to be machined.

In the early years of the war the yard was mainly involved in the construction of dredgers, tugs and corvettes. The acute shortage of naval escorts was partially met by the construction of the Flower Class Corvette, based on a whaler catcher design. These vessels were sometimes referred to as the 'cheap and nasties' because they were relatively inexpensive to build and yet proved deadly to many U-Boats. Of the 288 built in total, Alexander Hall built seven and Hall Russell built five. The *Marguerite*, built by Hall Russell in 1940, destroyed the U-Boat U-433 which was responsible for sinking the aircraft carrier *Ark Royal* in November 1941.

Although the two firms had similarities in their names and the yards lay adjacent to one another, they were in fact quite independent. A. Hall & Co. was established in 1790 and is probably best remembered for its development of the Aberdeen or Clipper Bow in 1839. This was designed in part as an aid to reducing the depth of a ship's hull (so avoiding unnecessary taxation – measured at the time by the depth of the hull) by extending the bow in a strengthened construction further forward above the waterline than was usual in contemporary design of the era. By default, this tax saving design led to a sleeker more efficient bow which proved to aid speed as well as seaworthiness. The company became responsible for many famous clippers such as *Torrington* and *Stornoway* which were built for speed and mainly plied the Far Eastern tea trade route (hence 'Tea Clipper'). Speed was of the essence on this route to bring tea to Europe as quickly as possible so as to beat the competition and command the best prices for the merchant in the fiercely competitive European tea market.

What perhaps many people don't know is that the most famous clipper of them all, the *Cutty Sark*, was not as fast as its greatest rival, the Aberdeen built *Thermopylae*, which was launched in 1868 and created her first record (still not beaten by a sailing ship) on her maiden voyage from England to Australia which she completed in 60 days.

However, by the early 1880s faster passages for the tea trade could be made by steamships, so the graceful clippers became employed in the less glamorous Australian wool trade. Nevertheless, the 'Aberdeen Line' fleet in general maintained a reputation across all their routes for style and class.

Although best known for sailing ships, A. Hall & Co. also constructed steamers. They built their first marine engine in 1887 for the launch vessel *Petrel*. In 1888 they constructed their first trawler, *Maggie Walker* and many trawlers, coasters, tugs and dredgers followed. However, the yard did not modernise after the war and in 1957 Hall Russell took over the company. They in turn had closed down by 1992 and it seems certain now that the industry of shipbuilding will never return to the Footdee location.

My working hours at the shipyard were 8–5.30, Monday to Friday, and 8–12 on a Saturday when we were paid. In my third year I was paid 10s 9d a week which was far from being a good wage, but good apprenticeships were valued in those days because of what they could lead to. Most of my pay went to my mother as I was still living at home with her. My father had died in February 1940 and my two sisters and my brother had all been married for several years. To put that wage in some sort of perspective, I can tell you that a pint of beer in those days cost 9d, so you don't need to be a mathematician to work out that frequenting pubs was virtually a non starter for those in my situation.

No tea breaks were allowed at the shipyards and you got one hour for your lunch. I usually went home for mine because it didn't cost me anything and I could cycle there in fewer than 10 minutes. If anyone was more than five minutes late in arriving for work, then they were docked at least half an hour's pay. This could be significant for a journeyman who did earn a good wage, and quite often workers who came over the former St Clements Bridge from the Torry side of the Harbour were penalised in this way. If the horn sounded at 8am and the dock gates were open, then they would suffer financially if they were stuck on the other side of the bridge.

Two of my fellow apprentices working on the surface table were Harold King and Innes Taylor. Harold was then a member of the auxiliary or weekend airforce and, by some coincidence, the three of us all ended up living in Dundee many years after the war and rekindled our friendship. Innes wrote a piece for the *Leopard* magazine in 1985 which gave an eyewitness account of the raid on 12 July 1940. He described how a box of glasses had landed outside the Neptune Bar and he slipped the only two unbroken ones, wrapped in tissue paper, into his pocket. He said that they were still raised each year on 12 July with mixed emotions. That day, you see, also happened to be his birthday.

Chapter 2
EARLY YEARS

When I was born on 30 April 1922 I was very much the baby of the family as my sister Maggie, brother Sandy and sister Muriel were then 14, eight and six respectively. At that time the family lived at 16 Jasmine Terrace which was, and still is, a mainly residential street running between the main thoroughfare of King Street and Park Street towards the beach. However, about four years after I was born we moved a couple of doors along to a second floor tenement flat at number 20 which comprised three rooms and share of an outside lavatory. That row of dwellinghouses has long been demolished and replaced with newer housing but the opposite side of the street remains much as it was then (the family had also stayed at number 57 for a spell before I was born).

My earliest memories are of my older sisters who, not surprisingly, had a major role in looking after me. I went to King Street Primary School (the entrance was off Urquhart Road) when I was five and in due course attended Frederick Street Intermediate School from the age of 12. Although I was only there for two years I remember that it was a tough school. On my very first day I got three of the belt or 'tawse' on each hand from Mr Ironside, the maths teacher, for shouting 'Here he comes' when I saw him approaching the classroom through the glass panel of the door.

When they weren't stinging from corporal punishment, I was pretty good with my hands and I remember the technical teacher, Mr Morgan, being impressed with my efforts. He sent one item I made – a Russian style clapper device for scaring crows – to an exhibition in Edinburgh.

My fascination with woodwork and metalwork was to get me into big trouble, however, when I was thirteen. One night I was playing 'Kick the Tin' with some pals which had an element of hide and seek in it. I hid in a granite yard which lay adjacent to the carpentry shop of Henderson, the large engineering company whose premises were on King Street. There I noticed a shed which was not locked and held a large electric motor. The belt from this went up a large inclined housing to a pulley inside the workshop. I managed to climb up this and then found that I could drop down into the joiner's workshop. I would like to think that this was through devilment and a sense of adventure rather than any serious criminal intent. Nonetheless, the fact is that after exploring the premises I took from each of the carpenters' tool boxes a small brass spokeshave. These were for planing small pieces of wood and, after leaving the premises, I hid them under a stairway. I told a couple of my pals about my escapade and gave one or two of the shaves to them. The next thing I knew, the police paid a visit to my parents and I found myself in court. At that time, the birch was a distinct possibility for certain categories of offence and indeed one of my pals, a lad called Billy Mortimer, had suffered this punishment. However, I was spared this, thanks in no small part to a new probation officer, Mr Taylor, who confirmed in court that he would take me under his wing. He had a small office at the Lads Club in the Gallowgate and I had to report to him once a week and also join the Club where I became involved in boxing among other things. He was very kind to me and also arranged for me to join the Boys Brigade 5th Company based in a church hall at the junction of West North Street and King Street. I really enjoyed my time with the BB, and in particular, the exercises on the gym apparatus, including the horse and parallel bars. I was also a dab hand at draughts as my father was an enthusiast and I competed successfully in competitions at junior level.

One sport I was keen on but sadly not gifted at, was football. Frederick Street had one of the strongest school teams in Aberdeen during my time there but I wasn't good enough to feature in it. However, I did watch Aberdeen FC at Pittodrie Park occasionally because my pals and I could often get in for free by getting someone to give us a 'liftie up' over the wall. The Dons had some great players during that era, including Willie Cooper, Matt Armstrong, Willie Mills and Jacky Benyon. However, my favourite was Billy Strauss, a South African winger who was very direct and had a terrific shot. Unfortunately, he was to miss the 1937 Cup Final against Celtic, when the Dons lost 2–1, because of an injury sustained in the semi against Morton.

* * * * *

As you can imagine my parents, in particular my father, gave me a deserved hard time in the aftermath of the Henderson break in, but eventually that died down. They had been married in 1907 and until I was about eight or nine my father, Charles, was employed as a hand compositor at Averys, the printers in King Street. He then went to work at Kirriemuir Free Press for a couple of years and only came home about once a month because he had to work weekends. He sent his overalls home to be washed and always enclosed a packet of 'starry rock' for me. This was a Kirriemuir speciality.

Following his return to Aberdeen around 1933 he worked for a spell with the Council digging trenches and I remember taking his lunchtime piece across to where he was working. By then he wasn't really fit enough for hard manual work and he was unemployed from about 1935 until his death some five years later at the age of 56, following an epileptic fit.

It is to this day a matter of regret for me that my father never once told me about his experiences during World War One, or the Great War as it was then known. My sisters told me later that he was in the 2nd and then the 4th Gordon Highlanders and that he had been badly wounded at Hill 60 in the

Ypres Salient. He then spent a lengthy convalescence in hospital in the north of Ireland and once he recovered he enlisted in the Royal Fusiliers. He was involved with transport in the Royal Fusiliers and I remember Muriel showing me photographs of him in uniform with horses. Sadly, those photographs and other memorabilia could not be found when she passed away in 1983. Accordingly, the only photograph I still have of my father is one with my mother Margaret on their wedding day.

After his enforced retirement, my father spent a lot of time reading and also at his plot on Seaton Road where I helped him on occasion. My sister, Maggie, was a weaver at Grandholm Mills until she moved to Portsmouth with her husband, Tom Rennie when he joined the Navy. My brother, Sandy, worked in a cycle repair shop near New Advocates Park and was married to Vera in 1934. By the time he enlisted in the Queen's Own Cameron Highlanders on the outbreak of war, he had four young daughters. Tragically he was killed in action in North Africa in June 1941.

Muriel's first job was at Pirie Appletons, the stationery manufacturer on Guild Street, and I remember her buying me a toy gun from her first wages. It cost 6d which was a lot of money for her and I was both delighted and astonished because money at home had been very tight. To get presents, even at Christmas and on birthdays, was virtually unknown. Muriel married Tom McCallum in 1935, so all my siblings had flown the nest by then.

The following year, 1936, I left school at the end of the summer term, having turned 14 and visited the Labour Exchange where I was offered a job as a pageboy at the Forsyth Hotel on Union Street. This later became the Gloucester Hotel and is now occupied by Peterkins, a firm of solicitors. At that time it was a temperance hotel and I was often asked to go round to the Prince of Wales pub in the lane behind the hotel to get half bottles for the guests. However, my main tasks were carrying luggage and cleaning duties such as the copper tables in the smoke room, which was a big job. 'Head Boots' was Alex Dilley, an ex-guardsman who had served in World War One and was a really nice man.

My pay at the Forsyth was a meagre 5s a week but the uniform was provided and I was able to take my meals there for free. I was also allowed to keep any tips which meant that my mother got the 5s, or, to be precise, 4s 10d after the deduction of 2d for the employment stamp. Any disposable income I had at that time was more often than not spent at the cinema which usually cost 4d. That was by far the most popular form of public entertainment in those days and most people went to the pictures at least two or three times a week. In 1938 Aberdeen had no fewer than 19 cinemas. I remember in particular the Regent (later the ABC), the Queens, the Picture House, the Belmont, the Majestic and the Capital, which were all on or around Union Street.

My mother looked after the house and was never in paid employment while I was living there. Although those were hard times, particularly after my father became unemployed, food was relatively cheap and I remember for example that you could get marvellous large mince pies for just one and a half pence at Bendelows (known as 'Bendies') at Causewayend. In fact, they were so popular that there was a ditty which included the words 'she's got eyes like Bendies pies'. With Aberdeen being a major fishing port, fish was always plentiful and most people knew someone who worked on the trawlers and could get free fish. In the mid 1930s there were 3,000 fishermen on 300 trawlers in Aberdeen and, even if you had to pay for them, at the height of the herring season you could buy eight herring for 1d. My mother showed remarkable versatility in the diverse ways she could cook these, including fried, baked and soused. Funnily enough I never tired of this staple in our diet.

My time at the Forsyth Hotel came to an end in May 1938 when I managed to obtain an apprenticeship at A. Hall & Co. courtesy of an introduction to the foreman by a good friend of mine, Harold Gordon, who was already employed there.

* * * * *

I mentioned previously that when war came, men in reserved occupations, such as myself, could not join the forces. However, in September 1941, when it was decreed that we could now volunteer for RAF aircrew (but not the army or the navy), one evening after work I hotfooted it down to the recruiting centre at Woolmanhill. Outside the passage leading to the office a blond youth was pacing to and fro. When I started up the passage, he called out 'Hey min, are you going to join the Air Force?' When I nodded, he said 'Wait, I'm coming with you'. I had already recognised him as he was the international table tennis champion, Victor Garland, and from then on we became good pals. Soon after, I got notice to attend for a medical examination and aptitude tests in Edinburgh. The test most dreaded by applicants was holding up a column of mercury for 60 seconds by blowing into a tube. The mercury had not to drop below a certain mark and the mouthpiece was designed so that you could not block it with your tongue. After half a minute, each tick of the second hand on the clock was excruciatingly long. By the time the minute was up, your lungs were bursting and your eyes were popping out of your head.

There was then a long wait for my call up papers and rail warrant, during time which I received dental treatment and preliminary instruction in navigation and morse code with a local training corps.

Chapter 3

I JOIN THE RAF

Eventually in mid February 1942 the buff envelope arrived. With great excitement I opened it and read that I was to report to the Air Crew Receiving Centre at Lords Cricket Ground in London the following week, a rail warrant being enclosed.

I remember well that freezing February day when I boarded the London train at the Joint Station, Aberdeen. Even though I had met the girl who I would eventually marry at a dance some weeks before, I wasn't unhappy that no one was there to wish me *bon voyage.* I had plenty to think about as I waited for the powerful A4 Class steam locomotive to pull the train away. It was indeed a great adventure for me because, apart from my RAF medical and tests at Edinburgh, until then the furthest I had travelled was to Dundee when I had cycled there one holiday weekend. I was 14 at the time, had one shilling in my pocket and tried to sleep in a telephone box. At 5am the next morning I cycled back to Aberdeen against a stiff headwind. When I had reached Stonehaven I was exhausted and tried to get a rail ticket for the last 16 miles to Aberdeen. However, the previous evening I had bought a pie and a cup of tea at the coffee stall in Dundee and only had 9d left. The rail ticket cost a shilling with another penny for the cycle and so, reluctantly, there was nothing else for it but to get on the saddle and push pedals for home.

On arriving at the ACRC at Lords Cricket Ground, we were 'kitted out'. You will find nothing comparable with 'kitting out'. Elderly men of indeterminate rank glared at us from behind a long counter. Some of them were so short-sighted they wore pebble glasses. But (and without the use of a single tape measure) they measured us, weighed us and within seconds reached a final conclusion, swiftly followed by hurling garments at us at chest height.

They chanted 'This, this, this, two of these, a pair of these. For Christ's sake catch 'em lad. I'm doing this for your benefit not mine'. By the time I reached the end of the counter I was in urgent need of a pack mule.

Then the corporal's 'Get those uniforms on, come on, come on, move. What do you mean it doesn't fit? Of course it bloody well fits...you'll grow into it. I don't give a damn what size you take in shoes...that's the size you take in boots! Gerrum on we'll soon work your feet into the right shape'.

After packing our civvies and spare garments into a kitbag, we were marched to Stockleigh Hall, St John's Wood. These were flats requisitioned by the RAF in Prince Albert Road, on the north side of Regents Park, having been the upmarket homes of affluent Londoners before becoming billets for budding air crew. The rooms had of course been stripped of all furnishings and valuable artefacts boarded off, resulting in plain, bare living spaces to be scrubbed and cleaned regularly and rigorously in the time honoured tradition. Each airman was involved, no consideration being given to the fact that he might be suffering from aching and swollen arms as a result of inoculations and vaccinations carried out at Abbey Lodge, the medical centre nearby.

Abbey Lodge was the first place I ever saw the phrase – 'Abandon hope all ye that enter here' – in this case scrawled over the door of a rear entrance where there were long queues. In the RAF, every flight or detachment was lined up in alphabetical order and therefore I found myself at the end of every queue of a flight of 50 men during those early years of training. One particular injection we had to endure was when the medical orderly pinched your chest and threw (!) a hypodermic needle in from the side. There were four needles on a tray and another orderly was filling them up as they were used. The actual needles were never changed for at least the 50 men in our squad and they burst in with a plop. I recall that the men who fainted were usually six footers, mostly ex-bobbies. Good job there was no Aids going about then!

Food, always a subject of importance to young airmen, was provided at Regents Park Zoo Restaurant. This entailed being lined up and being marched about three quarters of a mile to the entrance. For the evening meal and breakfast the front and rear offside men were given a white and red lamp respectively to carry. When it was discovered that the breakfast parade was not compulsory, the numbers dwindled away until only two of us, a Glaswegian named Jock Thompson and I, lined up at 6.30am. The corporal still insisted that we carry the white and red lamps which made us feel a bit foolish, but the very cold weather made us so hungry we would have been ravenous by lunchtime. When cocoa and biscuits were also served at 9.30pm, Jock and I were again the only takers from our flight. All the others seemed to have plenty of money and could buy themselves better suppers.

One of the serving orderlies at the Zoo canteen said to us, 'You lads shouldn't touch that cocoa, it's full of bromide'. When we asked 'What was bromide?' he said 'It kills your sex drive'. We both laughed and drank up our cocoa. There didn't seem to be much chance of our sex driving anywhere, so we might as well dampen it down a bit.

* * * * *

When we first arrived at Stockleigh Hall, Corporal Croswell, who was in charge of our flight, had said 'Gather round. Watch, learn and inwardly digest. This is how you will make up your bed. Every morning like this. No other way. I'm going to tell you once – and once only – and God help any man who makes a complete arse of it once he's been shown'. When we were all endeavouring to make a decent job of sandwiching the two folded white sheets between three blankets, then the fourth blanket folded round the lot, the corporal came over to Jock Thompson's bed, which was directly opposite mine, and said to him,

'It might interest you to know whose bed this was'. He then informed Jock that the previous occupant had been an aircrew cadet called Gordon Cummins. He had been arrested just days before for allegedly killing four women and attempting to murder two others in a spree lasting less than a week. He had also savagely mutilated his victims and this was to earn him the soubriquet 'The Blackout Ripper'.

Cummins first came to the attention of the public on 9 February 1942 when the body of Miss Evelyn Hamilton, a woman of irreproachable character, was found strangled in an air raid shelter in Marylebone. No sooner had the police come to terms with the fact that they had a vicious murderer to deal with than Cummins struck again, this time killing Evelyn Oakley, a prostitute, whose throat was cut and whose body was found in a Soho apartment the very next morning. His third victim was a 42-year-old woman, Mrs Lowe, whose mutilated body was not discovered until three days later. Cummins struck again that same night, picking up and killing a prostitute named Mrs Jouannet, this time making his escape by means of a fire exit.

On Friday 14 February he picked up a Mrs Greta Heywood and took her for a drink at the famous Trocadero in Piccadilly. He then assaulted her in a doorway on Haymarket, but she fought back and Cummins was scared off by the intervention of an errand boy who had heard the struggling pair. Seeing him approaching, Cummins fled into the night, leaving behind his gas mask with his name, rank and number on it. Even this didn't seem to deter him, for within a few hours he had returned to the West End where he picked up his next intended victim, a young prostitute named Mrs Mulcahy, and they went by taxi to her apartment in Southwick Street in the Paddington area.

After entering the flat Cummins grabbed her by the throat but she managed to kick him hard on the shins, causing him to release his grip on her throat. Strangely, he seemed to then panic and left the flat in a hurry, having pressed some money into her hand.

By this time the police had been able to trace him through his gas mask to his billet in Stockleigh Hall. However, the investigating officer, DI Greeno, was faced with a problem which held up his enquiries. Cummins's name in the billet pass book showed that he was in at the times the murders had taken place and, if this was correct, then he must be innocent. It was not until DI Greeno found out that the pass book was regularly altered by the other airmen in the billet to cover for one another's absences, that everything fell into place and Cummins was formally charged and arrested shortly before we arrived at Stockleigh Hall.

We did not hear any more of Gordon Cummins during the course. All of the previous intake of which he was a member had passed on to the ITW (Initial Training Wing) so there was no one to discuss with us Cummins's characteristics. That is except for our corporal of course, but apart from telling Jock that he was occupying the bed of an alleged murderer, he never volunteered any further information about him.

In the event, Cummins was duly convicted and executed at Wandsworth Prison on 25 July 1942. The trial at the Old Bailey did not get the press coverage it would have done if there had not been a war on. As for us, we were too concerned with the examinations we had to undergo. Apart from the medical, there were maths exams, aptitude tests, essays, etc. etc. We were still liable to be thrown off the course for pilot & observer and have to remuster as other aircrew if we failed. As it happened I was to benefit from a monumental posting cock-up which came about as follows.

A large proportion of our flight of 50 men had come straight from universities and maths exams to them were a 'piece of cake', but to some of us who had left school at the age of 14, it was a struggle. Approaching the end of the three week course at ACRC we had all been assessed and graded. The top 25, the real clever dicks, were erroneously posted to Brighton for a 'maths refresher course' and the rest of us were posted to Number 13 Initial Training Wing at Torquay. I heard later that when they realised what had happened their complaints were ignored and they still had to do their three weeks of maths instructions with further examinations at the end of it.

* * * * *

It was about this time I heard from my mother that my brother Sandy was reported missing believed killed. Later it was confirmed that he had been killed in Operation Battleaxe at Halfaya Pass in Egypt on 15 June 1941.

The goal of Operation Battleaxe was to clear eastern Cyrenaica (the eastern coastal region of modern Libya) of German and Italian forces, one of the main benefits of which would be the lifting of the siege of Tobruk. By the end of May 1941 the Greek island of Crete had fallen to the Germans. This meant that the Luftwaffe would have additional airfields available to threaten allied shipping and also to protect their own supply convoys and troops in Cyrenaica. To offset this the British chiefs of staff made it clear to General Archibald Wavell, Commander in Chief, Middle East, that it was imperative that control be wrested from the Axis forces in the area between Sollum and Derna and that British air forces in that region be thus re-established.

Accordingly Wavell launched the attack on 15 June. The plan was to hold attention at Halfaya Pass, south east of Sollum, with one column while others were sent against Sollum, Fort Capuzzo and the German base at Sidi Aziez. The operation did not succeed though, as the initial assaults by the British forces came up against strong defensive positions created by German general Erwin Rommel.

My brother's infantry battalion of the Queen's Own Cameron Highlanders were part of the 'Coast Force' which was charged with capturing Halfaya Pass. They were positioned on top of the escarpment with 13 Matilda tanks of the 4th Royal Tank Regiment and an artillery battery which was scheduled to open fire at 5.40am on the German and Italian forces stationed in Halfaya to provide cover for the tanks and infantry. However, the battery became bogged down by soft sand and after waiting until 6am, the tank commander ordered his tanks to attack at the top of the pass. Soon after though the anti-tank guns of the German and Italian defences opened fire and within a few hours the Matildas had all been destroyed. The Camerons initially continued their advance but were soon driven back by a detachment of German armoured cars and motorised infantry and it is believed that Sandy was killed at some point during this stage of the proceedings.

The British lost over half of their total number of tanks on the first day and only achieved limited success at one of their three thrusts. They were then gradually pushed back and only narrowly avoided outright disaster on the third day by withdrawing just ahead of a German encircling movement which would have cut them off from retreat.

The utter failure of the operation led to the replacement of Wavell by General Claude Auchinleck. With the British forces defeated and with no available reserves, Egypt lay wide open to Rommel. However, his critical supply position and the continuing threat to his rear from the Tobruk garrison prevented him from attempting to exploit his success.

Although my brother was eight years older than me and left home when I was quite young, I still felt his loss keenly. With my father not long dead and my brother now gone I was now the only surviving male member of the family. His body, along with many others, was never recovered and his name is remembered with honour on Column 72 of the Alamein Memorial in Egypt.

At the time of the Battleaxe debacle the British Empire was in dire straits, with the Germans seemingly on their way to defeating us in North Africa, having already forced us out of France and Norway. The Russians were on the ropes, America was demanding (and getting) most former British possessions in the western hemisphere in exchange for a few clapped out four stacker destroyers and the news arriving from the Far East was that 350,000 British troops in 'Fortress Singapore' had just surrendered to about a 10th of that number of Japanese soldiers, many mounted on bicycles. Have you ever seen the famous photographs of that event? – almost as humiliating as the fact that we were surrendering, were the appalling shorts our generals wore in order to surrender.

* * * * *

Arriving at Torquay at the end of March, we were billeted at the Rosetor Hotel and that's when our training really started. An officer and a corporal were in charge of us, the pilot officer being an insignificant type, short and tubby with a thin moustache. He bore the insignia of the educational branch on his lapels – the torches of learning. Our corporal, however, was a strict disciplinarian and it was his dedication to his job that really licked us into shape.

Reveille was at 6am followed by, rain or shine, a three mile run finishing with a swim in the sea. Then breakfast followed firstly by parade and inspection and then two hours drill. We were highly amused by a collie dog which invariably joined us at drill sessions. I don't know if he was a retired sheepdog but he always snapped at the heels of Corporal Manning, probably trying to shoo him in with all the other blue sheep. We all came to like and respect the corporal and secretly warmed to him, for never once did he lose his temper with that dog.

After the morning drills came lectures on navigation, morse code, aircraft recognition, gunnery, Kings regulations, etc. etc. After lunch practical application was given to the foregoing lectures. Every Wednesday we went on a route march of approximately 18 miles with full pack and only a packet of sandwiches and our water bottles. By the time we got back to our evening meal we were all ravenous. Pay parades every fortnight were welcome. You had to step up to the table, salute, shout your last three numbers, scoop (in my case 14 shillings) into your left hand, step back and salute the pay officer again, then march off.

Being short of money most of the time turned out to my advantage. The other impecunious cadets and I spent our evenings in the morse code room, practising sending and receiving messages. At the end of the course the examination requirement was eight words per minute but I could send and receive 14wpm without thinking and, in fact, 8wpm became a drag.

I was also fortunate in having no trouble reading the Aldis Lamp. About 25 per cent of the chaps just could not read the flashing light and subsequently at the end of ITW were delayed in being promoted to LAC (Leading Aircraftsman) until they reached Elementary Flying Training School. This meant being deprived of flying pay (which was 7s 6d a day) for about five weeks which was a lot of money then.

Jock Thompson was one of the unfortunates who could not read the Aldis Lamp, but as we were teamed together I read the test message for him and he passed. Although I was not proud of being an accessory to cheating, Jock and I had apportioned half our basic pay to our mothers, both widows, and we were always strapped for cash. His delight on our first big pay parade eased my conscience.

* * * * *

Returning from leave in mid June we were posted to Wolverhampton Municipal Aerodrome, Elementary Flying Training School. Here we were tested and graded in Tiger Moth biplane aircraft.

Of all the Aerodromes I have ever been stationed at or visited, this one had the best camouflage I had ever seen. From outside the camp it just looked like grassy slopes. The work was still in progress and young women were pleating green material on wires suspended above the huts. Long planks straddled the wires and the girls worked as a team shifting and pleating. One of our first parades on arriving was an FFI (free from infection) and we were lined up in our respective barracks and had to drop our pants while the Medical Officer came along and gave us the once over. The pleating squad were right above us and would have had a good view through the windows but the MO said 'Never mind the women, they are too busy to look at you lot'. We were all embarrassed and I am sure the way the girls were all giggling and laughing was not their normal banter.

It reminded me of the joke about the Gordon Highlander regiment who were undergoing an FFI parade. The MO stopped in front of one 'old sweat' and hoping to incur some amusement in the proceedings, lifted up the soldier's 'willie' on the end of his cane and said 'I bet this bird has been in many a nest', to which the old sweat replied 'Yes sir, but it's the first time it's been on a perch'.

My first ever flight was on 25 June. I went up first for 30 minutes to gain experience with a Sergeant Frost, then after about an hour I went up again for

45 minutes with another Sergeant Pilot Instructor and was allowed to handle the controls. For the next 11 days, if the weather was suitable, we were put through the gamut of flying exercises – straight and level, climbing, gliding, stalling, medium turns, tight turns, spinning, gliding approaches and landings. The final flight was a test with the Chief Flying Instructor Flight Lieutenant Ellis.

Some of the cadets were washed out before the final test because of incompatibility. Sadly, Jock Thompson was one of the unfortunates who failed and was posted with the other washouts to an air gunnery school. It was nearly two years later when I heard that he had been killed while flying as a rear gunner with Bomber Command.

All of us who completed the grading course were then posted to the aircrew holding unit at Heaton Park, Manchester. Most of us did not know if we would be carrying on training as a pilot or navigator. As I was one of those who did not go solo, although it was bad weather that prevented me from being sent up on my own, at that time I was not unduly worried about carrying on as a navigator. I had quite taken to navigation exercises and would have gladly accepted that role if I had not passed for a pilot. I know that navigators have an absorbing and extremely satisfying job. That is, if they are good at it. Eventually I was to qualify for my navigator's diploma at the General Reconnaissance School at Charlottetown, Prince Edward Island, Canada. Nonetheless it was still a great feeling when the lists were posted as to who was to carry on training as pilots or navigators and I saw that my name was on the former list.

CHAPTER 4

NORTH AMERICA BOUND

Heaton Park in Manchester was the last dispersal unit for would-be aircrew destined to continue training overseas where the weather would be more suitable. I arrived there about mid July 1942 along with several hundred others. It was a huge area with trees concealing hundreds of dispersed huts, each one containing about 20 hopefuls.

We were there for about six weeks and before every mealtime we were marched to the dining hall in a mansion on high ground to the accompaniment of *The Airforce March* and *Rhythm Saved the World* relayed through a powerful address system.

Although we had drills and lectures the programme was not nearly as hectic as the initial training at Torquay had been and we were free to go into Manchester every evening. However, anyone coming in the guard gates after midnight was put on a charge and had to do 'jankers' (drills with full pack) and also cookhouse duties. Unsurprisingly, therefore, the number of men coming back over the wall was considerable. Our hut though was near a culvert which ran out of the grounds through a tunnel about four feet high and the water was usually only about four inches deep with plenty of brick stepping stones. Accordingly we normally used this route unless there had been a lot of rain, in which case we too came back over the wall.

One afternoon in late August hundreds of us were mustered after frantic organisation and transported to the rail depot. After an all night journey with frequent long stoppages and umpteen shuntings on to different railtracks we arrived in Gourock on the Firth of Clyde at the crack of dawn. As we queued with our kit bags to board the tender ship we could see the huge troopship in battleship grey a couple of miles offshore. It was a surprise when the tender passed astern and we saw the letters, *QUEEN ELIZABETH*. The great ship had lost a lot of its good looks with its drab war paint.

Once aboard, I was allocated one of eight bunks, which had been installed in one of the expensive A class cabins. Apart from the hundreds of aircrew cadets and Canadian soldiers returning with their wounded comrades, the ship was comparatively empty. It would be a different story when I was to return in a year's time on the *Queen Mary*.

After the wartime rations the food on board was marvellous. There were only two mealtimes per day but the tables were laden with almost everything that was either rationed or unobtainable in wartime Britain. All kinds of fruit, bowls of boiled eggs, white bread, etc. etc. Also the ship's store was selling all kinds of chocolates, sweets and cigarettes but no alcohol.

On the second morning out we were surprised to see the ship's officers in their white uniforms while we were uncomfortably warm in our heavy blue uniforms. Then we found out that we were nearly in the tropics to avoid the German submarine wolf packs that were lying in wait in the North Atlantic. It was fascinating to watch the numerous flying fish scurrying away from the ship's bow cutting through the water at nearly 30 knots.

The voyage took four and a half days until in brilliant sunshine we sailed slowly in to New York. I, along with many others, climbed the foremast rigging to get a better view. I fully expected that the loudspeaker system would blast out an order for us to get down but looking back to the bridge, the captain and all his officers were smiling broadly.

Once the ship had docked, no time was wasted before we disembarked and had entrained for the long journey to Moncton, New Brunswick. We travelled for hour after hour through the American and then the Canadian countryside with the trees just starting to get their famous autumn colouring. Once darkness fell I remember the first Canadian town we stopped at with its brightly lit shop windows and the displays of fresh fruit, sights almost forgotten in blacked out and rationed Britain.

By midnight most of the novelty had given way to tiredness and the station sign of Moncton, our destination, was a welcome sight. Located in Westmorland County, New Brunswick, Moncton lies at the geographic centre of the maritime provinces and had the nickname 'Hub City' because it had historically been the railway and land transportation hub for the maritime provinces of Nova Scotia, New Brunswick and Prince Edward Island, bordering on the Atlantic Ocean. It was named after Brigadier Robert Monckton, the British Officer who was second in command to General James Wolfe at the victorious Siege of Quebec in 1759 which effectively ended France's hold on our North American colonies.

After more hauling of kitbags and climbing on and off transport vehicles we arrived at the RAF Base at Moncton, through which all British personnel destined for flying training in Canada and the USA passed.

After a welcome meal there was an even more welcome pay parade, each man receiving one crisp 10 dollar note and a one dollar note. We were then allocated beds in the wooden huts where, dog-tired, everyone fell fast asleep in seconds at around 3am.

* * * * *

We hadn't long at Moncton before embarking on another long rail journey, this time taking us to the American Navy flying training base at Grosse Ile in the state of Michigan. Grosse Ile is the largest island in the Detroit River which is a 32 miles long strait travelling south from Lake St Clair to Lake Erie and the whole river carries the international border between Canada and the United States.

In August 1941, some four months before the Japanese attack on Pearl Harbour, the base had started a slightly new mission, the primary flight training of British aviation cadets. The previous day to our arrival, two British air cadets had been killed in an air collision and so, after settling in, our first parade the next day was the funeral and service for our two comrades.

We were now to begin training at one of the world's toughest navy flying schools where 50 per cent of our course and most other courses were washed out. Those that did not wash out would go on to Pensacola in Florida to complete their flight training. It would be eight months later after rigorous flying training with numerous checks and exams before the survivors earned the right to wear a pair of the coveted RAF wings.

My first instructor was a Lieutenant Morton with whom I got on very well and our first flight in the old Northrop 1 open cockpit biplane was on 29 September 1942. Then after six more flights with him I was transferred to a Lieutenant Breitner* who for some reason took an immediate and intense dislike to me and screamed and shouted at me in the air if I made the slightest misjudgement. He was of German descent but it was not that he was anti-British because his other pupil was English and he was always smiling and chatting with him, even inviting him to his home on occasion.

It was because of Breitner that I was very late in going solo. His favourite pupil had not got the aptitude for flying and so Breitner tried very hard for him to go solo before I did. When he knew he could not hold me back any further he put me forward for my 'A' check and a Lieutenant Sekulski took me up. Bad weather intervened and cut the check flight short but Sekulski told me that he had seen enough and he considered that I was fit to go solo.

Next day the weather cleared and I expected a quick check by an instructor before getting up on my own but to my surprise I was listed for an hour and a half solo in Northrop 1- 3671. I wasted no time and sprinted to the aeroplane

* Not his real name.

and then took off as quickly as possible. I had a marvellous time and, getting well away from the vicinity of the airfield, I indulged myself in aerobatics, low flying and spending very little time on the exercises that I was supposed to be doing.

Landing and taxiing to the aircraft line up in front of the Flight Office, I could see Breitner waiting for me with a look of thunder on his face. As I walked in carrying my parachute, in front of the other instructors and pupils, he shouted, almost screamed in fact 'Yule, you are in real trouble, why did you go off on your own? You must have known you had to get a check circuit'. I replied 'There is nothing on the board about a check circuit, Sir. I fully trust the US Navy administration not to make a cock up'. The other instructors were laughing so he must have thought better than to pursue the issue and without another word he turned on his heel and strode away.

It was still very unpleasant flying with Breitner but since going solo I only had him for 90 minutes after which I had two periods of 90 minutes on my own before getting him again. The 2 November 1942 marked my first solo flight in the famous Stearman. This classic American trainer was an open cockpit biplane which was superb for aerobatics and the most enjoyable aircraft I have ever flown. Apart from Breitner, life was great on the camp with great food and good pay because the British cadets got the same pay as the lowest rank in the American Navy. Our kit was US Navy khaki with the only item of RAF clothing being our caps. There were top class shows and films laid on once a week and my new pal, funnily enough another Thompson, but this time an Englishman called Paul from Saffron Walden, was a great pianist and used to play before the show started. Playing all the popular songs of the period he always got a great ovation.

Flying was second nature to me now and I was passing all checks with no problem at all. This was not because of Breitner but in spite of him. I don't want to go on about him but in my whole life I am sure I have never been disliked by anyone so much. The puzzling thing about it was that I did not know why he hated me from the start when I had certainly not done anything to offend him.

Finally we finished the course at Grosse Ile, my last flight ever in the marvellous Stearman being on 2 February 1943. We were then granted eight days' leave before departing for Pensacola and the final leg of our training in America.

A lot of our course went to Chicago for their leave but Paul and I travelled the much longer distance to New York. This was the greatest leave I have ever had in the forces and apart from paying one dollar a night at the Plymouth Hotel everything else was free. We lined up every morning at the Civil Defence Centre along with American servicemen in different queues for tickets to shows. The premiere of *Random Harvest* with Greer Garson and Ronald Colman was one of the films we saw at the Radio City. We also had trips to the Empire State Building, Statue of Liberty, Coney Island and Jack Benny's live radio show. Also the famous *Stage Door Canteen* where Sophie Tucker was the visiting star that night (the previous night it had been Betty Grable).

On 18 February we entrained at Detroit for Pensacola, the naval equivalent of the US Army's West Point. The journey south took two days and the change of climate in so short a time was remarkable, leaving in arctic conditions and arriving in almost tropical heat in Florida. A naval bus met us at the railway station and transported us to the US Naval Air Station. On arriving we were amazed at the massive entrance gates that let us into what can only be described as an aviation city. There were massive buildings with four airfields for land planes and three waterways for seaplanes and flying boats. The base covered thirty square miles and had an internal bus service with appropriate bus stops that included a map and service timetables. We were told that civilian personnel numbered thirty thousand but no figures were given for service personnel for security reasons.

There was a shopping centre like a large supermarket where you could buy almost everything. There were also several restaurants and a cinema which could compete with anything in the UK, being completely air-conditioned and having a change of programme three times a week. Later on our course Bob Hope did a live radio show after which his entourage gave a marvellous one hour show. However, this was certainly no long holiday for us because apart from the heavy flying programme we had to swot up on American Navy navigation, wireless and seamanship with, finally, stiff exams on each.

We were billeted four to a room in very comfortable quarters. The food was excellent and served to us by waiters. In the 'Ship's Service' one could buy meals at any time and there was a library, a gym and an outdoor swimming pool.

On 23 February 1943 I started flying in the Valiant which was a low-winged monoplane with a fixed undercarriage and a more powerful engine than we had flown before. It had flaps which had to be wound up and down by hand and a two speed propeller. The course consisted mainly of formation flying which was very enjoyable and finished on 7 March. This was followed by a course on the Harvard aircraft which was not so enjoyable. It was mostly under the hood with an instructor, purely instrument flying and radio beam flying. This course finished on 2 April with a final check after which we received a certificate stating that we had passed the test in Instrument Flying prescribed for pilots of the United States Navy.

With those two flying courses behind me I could now look forward to the most exciting part of my training – flying the big 'Cats' of the US Navy, the Catalina Flying Boats. This was one of the finest flying boats ever built which served the world over in military and commercial guises. Every flight was a pleasure, even flying with our instructor, Flight Lieutenant Gibson, one of several RAF ex-coastal Command pilots who had taken over our training. Paul Thompson, another pal Brian Sellars and I elected to form a crew (each crew of three flew together for the remainder of the course) and the entire training became a pleasure rather than a bind. On dual instructions, when we weren't 'up front', we relaxed in one of the rear compartments but we thoroughly enjoyed ourselves when the three of us flew 'solo', so to speak. I remember one time when we landed in an inlet, turned off the engines, stripped and dived off the wings into the lovely cool water.

Our last flight on the Catalinas was on 26 May by which time we were considered to be competent pilots. On 11 June I was part of a Graduation Parade where the band played, we marched and the RAF and Fleet Air Arm students were presented with their wings as well as the Golden Wings of the US Navy. The American students also received their Golden Wings. We then celebrated with a few days leave in New Orleans.

We were all sorry to leave Pensacola which must have been one of the best, if not the best, service stations in the world. The USA certainly treated its armed forces well. We travelled north in a Pullman carriage with pull down beds and first class meals. Entering Canada we changed into a dirty old carriage and had to sleep in our seats. No meals were provided and we had to dash out at a station stop and buy a sandwich if there was a kiosk.

Finally we got back to Moncton again and much to our disappointment we discovered that we were not to return to Britain yet. Instead we had to endure a General Reconnaissance Course at Charlottetown, Prince Edward Island, which would elevate us to the role of Pilot/Observer. Our Navigation Course on Prince Edward Island started in earnest on 10 July and it was an extremely hard slog. When not in classrooms or out in the evenings carrying out astro navigation star shots, we climbed into Anson aircraft and navigated for three and a half to four hours each trip. Finally on 20 September after stiff exams on navigation, meteorology, ship recognition, aircraft recognition and more, we finished the course and awaited transport back to Moncton. In the meantime Paul Thompson had left to return to England and I lost touch with him after that. However, in the mid 1970s I was invited to a reunion for former Pensacola aircrew students held in London and was delighted to meet Paul and his wife Pat there. It transpired that he had become a Mosquito pilot and after the war had joined the Foreign Office. His job entailed a lot of travelling around and he said he didn't even have a piano any more because of the frequent moves of house. That seemed a waste because believe me he was a truly talented musician. Paul has sadly since passed away but I spoke to Pat on the phone for a while not long ago.

I met a girl at a dance in Charlottetown and she invited me to meet her family who were very welcoming. It turned out that she also had close relatives in Moncton and she came there to see me as well. I got the impression her family were quite taken with the idea of her getting hitched to a Scotsman as they had Scottish ancestry themselves. One incident I remember is her uncle, I think it was, returning home with a huge black bear tied to the bumper of his truck and telling us that he had no option but to shoot it. However, any prospects of a serious romance were doomed as I was due to get the boat back to Britain soon and apart from anything else I was hopeful that there might still be a girl waiting for me in Aberdeen.

CHAPTER 5

HOME ON THE *QUEEN MARY*

In late September 1943 I sailed back across the Atlantic, on this occasion on the *Queen Mary* along with over 12,000 other troops and airmen. With a crew of 863 this was just over 13,000 people on board but she had previously carried 15,125 plus 863 crew, nearly 16,000, on 2 August 1942.

We boarded at night in Halifax, Nova Scotia, which was the only time that the *Queen Mary* sailed from there during the war with troops, as she normally did so from New York. The liner's berthing capacity was 12,500 standee bunks some five deep. I had the middle of a three tier one in a low part of the deck. It was certainly not a luxury cruise. Changing into pyjamas at night and sleeping on a six by two feet canvas with a kitbag alongside my legs for five nights was quite an experience. The *Queen Mary* on her zigzag course over the North Atlantic rolled far worse than on the trip over to New York on the *Queen Elizabeth* the previous year. My bunk lay amidships and it was a continuous 30 degrees up on your neck, then 30 degrees up on your feet all night but, amazingly, you got accustomed to it and did sleep. There were only two meals a day but the food was very good. The main restaurant became the main mess hall and in place of 800 peacetime diners, 2,000 troops could be fed at one sitting.

On good weather days the aft decks became crowded with troops getting fresh air but there was no room for exercise. Life jackets had to be worn at all times. Even in peacetime the *Queen Mary* rolled badly and the crew would say 'she could roll the milk out of a cup of tea'. On her wartime 'GI shuttle' the *Queen Mary* maintained a number eight zigzag, which involved four minutes steaming on a mean (straight) course then a 25 degree turn to starboard for four minutes, 50 degrees port for eight minutes, then a 25 degree starboard for four minutes and then a 25 degree port turn took her back to her mean course. On the 50 degree port turn she really heeled over and a great roar went up as we on the starboard side seemed to be skimming the water, compared to those on the port side who to us were way up in the sky.

Apart from the foregoing pastime the troops indulged themselves in several activities which were not to the liking of either Cunard or the authorities – among these were playing dice (craps was a great favourite) and, as far as the ship's company was concerned, the chewing of gum was unpopular, being difficult to clean off the bulkheads and decks, as was the carving of initials on the teak wood handrails. The latter was eventually tolerated and as Captain Bisset later wrote, 'I decided not to make a fuss about this. These men might soon be going into battle and some of them would never return to their homes and loved ones. Let them amuse themselves, these carvings would later become treasured relics'.

We did not even glimpse any of the VIPs or brass hats on board but one celebrity who travelled during the war should be mentioned. This was a gentleman who travelled under the pseudonym 'Colonel Warden'. He travelled three times on the *Queen Mary*, partly because of being infected with tuberculosis on one occasion which prevented him from flying. He always travelled with a large retinue and used the chance of sailing in the Cunarder to make several important decisions. The *Queen Mary* had to wait for him on one occasion for 18 days to rejoin her and he was always appreciative of her crew and qualities. Cabins were even refurbished especially for his use. The man in question was Winston Churchill.

We did hear a rumour that the previous year the *Queen Mary* had been involved in an accident, but it was a well kept secret that remained until the end of World War Two. While I was arriving in New York on the *Queen Elizabeth* in late September 1942, the *Queen Mary* had departed on its shuttle run to Gourock on the Firth of Clyde. On these high speed GI shuttles across the Atlantic a cruiser would meet the *Queen Mary* off the north coast of Ireland to escort her through the potentially dangerous waters off the coast of Scotland. The escorting cruiser would act as an anti-aircraft ship and six destroyers would provide anti-submarine cover.

On 2 October 1942, HMS *Curacao* the 4,200 ton light cruiser that had been sent as an escort vessel, saw the smoke of the *Queen Mary* appear above the horizon. Accordingly she turned about and started at full speed towards the Scottish coast, knowing that even at the cruiser's full speed the *Queen Mary* would soon catch up and overhaul her. The *Queen Mary* maintained her zigzag course and the Curacao got in rather close. Later, witnesses said that an officer on the cruiser's bridge was taking photographs and was told 'You'll never get a better picture'. What happened next has long been a matter of debate. The *Curacao* should have been watching the *Queen Mary* very carefully but somehow she manoeuvred in too close alongside the *Queen Mary's* starboard side and, either a wrong helm order was given or else, as was suggested later by tank model experiments, the interaction between the two vessels pulled the cruiser in front of the rushing knife edge of the *Queen Mary's* bow. People on the *Queen Mary* either felt nothing, or a slight jolt or else they believed they were being bombed as the liner's bow knifed through the cruiser at 26 knots.

The time was 14:10 hours and during the awful moments which followed the cruiser's stern sank quickly, followed a few minutes later by the bow. Those brief moments of disaster claimed the lives of 331 officers and men, only 101 surviving the tragedy, the cruiser's Commanding Officer Captain John Boutwood being among the latter. In spite of the anguish of those witnessing the event from on board the *Queen Mary*, the liner could not stop. She could not risk the lives of the 15,000 crew and passengers by attempting a rescue in waters known to be frequented by U-Boats. To stop could easily court a greater catastrophe. Horrified troops on the *Queen Mary's* decks threw life jackets overboard as her mighty bulk steamed through the wreckage of ship and men. She notified the escort destroyers which then sped to rescue those thrashing about in the oily water.

The troopship's speed was reduced by half to 14 knots. Her bow had been split to the height of the cruiser's weather deck and also, fortunately, had been forced back and to one side as she cut through the warship thus sealing the huge wound in the damaged stem. Water entered the ship but its force of ingress was reduced as the ship slowed. The forward collision bulkhead held and was stiffened by the hurriedly applied wooden shores on the after side. The liner made Gourock safely, leaving many observers on shore wondering what had happened. They would be left wondering for a long time as the accident was hushed up until after the war when, after a series of inquiries, appeals, claims and counterclaims, blame for the incident was apportioned one-third to the *Queen Mary* and two-thirds to the *Curacao*, mainly for negligent watch keeping. The *Queen Mary's* Captain, Gordon Illingworth, normally an unassuming man, was to be frequently haunted by the incident in the years to come.

The crumpled bow of the super liner was temporarily patched up with cement and she returned to the States at around 24 knots, her speed still her best defense against U-Boats. She dry docked in Boston where a new stem section had been constructed from templates rushed over from Britain. So the *Queen Mary* continued to shuttle American troops to Britain, eventually in preparation for D-Day and its aftermath.

My journey on her ended when she sailed into Liverpool and after disembarking I was taken to a holding unit in Harrogate. We stayed in hotels there for a couple of weeks before I got to go on leave back to Aberdeen. It was the first time I had been home in almost 15 months and although I stayed with my mother as usual the priority for me was meeting up with my girlfriend

Winnie again. I gave her loads of Hersheys chocolate which I had brought back from America and which was in short supply in Britain. As I recall, we spent much of our time going to the cinema or dancing at the Palais in Diamond Street before, all too soon, it was time for me to return to Harrogate.

For all the availability of luxury items in the US and Canada, one thing that sticks in my mind about Harrogate were the huge queues formed by aircrew at the fish and chip shops. As they say, you can't beat a good fish supper, and that was one thing you didn't get over the pond.

Shortly after getting back to Harrogate I was transferred along with the rest of my squad of 50 men to Number 6 PAFU (Pilots Advanced Flying Unit) at Little Rissington, north west of Oxford. For the next four months we undertook flying, navigation and beam approach training on Oxfords, which were a twin-engined training plane. Amy Johnson, the famous air woman who made the first solo flight by a woman from England to Australia, was killed when the Oxford she was flying came down in the Thames Estuary on 5 January 1941 while she was serving in the Air Transport Auxiliary.

While I waited for a posting to an operational unit in Bomber Command, I was latterly the only test pilot for the Oxfords at both Little Rissington and Chipping Norton as all the others in my squad had by then been posted. On one day, 5 April 1944, I tested no fewer than 11 of these aircraft on my own, spending a good 30 minutes in the air each time. I am not sure why I came to be the last one left there but if I hadn't been available to do it then the only other qualified pilot would have been the officer in charge of the station. However, after my last test flight in an Oxford at Chipping Norton on 6 April I was finally moved to the Operational Training Unit at Lindholme near Doncaster.

Chapter 6

CREWING UP

A Wellington bomber hummed overhead in the clear morning air. It was the 12 April 1944, as I stood among the other pilots gathered at Lindholme and looked around the assembled groups of aircrew. There were bomb-aimers, navigators, wireless-operators and gunners and I needed one of each of the former and two of the latter to form my crew. I did not know any of them as up till now pilots had peopled my Air Force world. This was a crowd of strangers. I needed five of these men to fly with, live with and go to war with. If, as I fully expected by now, we went from Wellington bombers to four engine heavy bombers I would have to find an engineer later in our training. However, the six of us who came together now would form the nucleus of the crew.

I had not realised that the crewing up procedure would be so haphazard. If I had known it was going to be like this I would have given it some previous thought, but I imagined that the procedure would be just as impersonal as most others that we went through in the RAF. I had expected to simply see an order on the notice board detailing who was crewed with whom but what happened was quite different. When we had all paraded in the hangar, and the roll had been called, the Chief Ground Instructor got up on a dais. He wished us good morning, told us we were there for crewing up, and said 'right chaps, sort yourselves out'. He then jumped off the dais and left us to get on with it.

I decided to concentrate on the navigator first and directed my attention to a group of navigators. But how was I to pick one? I could not assess his aptitude with map and dividers from his face. Just then I saw two Australians looking at me, one tall, the other short. They walked over and the tall one spoke, 'we are looking for a pilot'. I held out my hand, 'Roy Yule'. 'I'm Stan Moore and this is Bob Grey*, he is the navigator. I am a navigator but have re-mustered as a bomb-aimer'. Bob then spoke, 'have you got a wireless-operator? I know a real good one, he comes from Sydney, I'll fetch him for you'.

While I was talking to Stan, two gunners came over, one slim, the other chunky. Slim spoke with a smile, 'want two good gunners?' He turned out to be Frank Fathers from Sheffield and chunky was Arthur Clayton from Wragby near Lincoln.

Bob Grey then returned with Greg Mayes the wireless-op., and we decided to go for a cup of tea. As we walked over to the canteen I realised that I had not made one single conscious choice.

* * * * *

There followed three weeks in ground school before we started flying in Wellingtons. We operated from the grass aerodrome at the satellite station of Bircotes while the runways at Finningley were getting resurfaced. Whenever an aircraft was serviceable we pounded the circuit and neighbouring air space doing dual and solo, overshoots and landings, with flap and without, single engine flying, cross country and practice bombing, and air firing and beam approach. Then we started the whole lot again at night.

On the night of 24 May an incident happened which was to spoil my promotion prospects. The runways at Finningley had just been completed and we were transferred there to fly that night. I had already completed four hours solo night flying at Bircotes from grass runways and with one single line of

* Not his real name.

paraffin flare lamps as the only airfield illumination. That night I was detailed for a check circuit and landing with Pilot Officer Perry, a screen pilot instructor.

We took off in Wellington E-292. It was a pitch-black night with 10/10ths overcast cloud at 1,500ft base. The control tower was having trouble with their R/T and their transmissions were unreadable but Perry had assumed clearance was granted. I circled the airfield and called up for permission to land. The reply from control was garbled and unreadable but Perry nodded for me to go in. I carried on downwind, made two turns on to the approach path and landed.

While we taxied round the perimeter track Perry tried, unsuccessfully, to get control to send out the vehicle with the compressed air cylinders to top up our braking system. The pressure gauge was reading only 30 psi when it should have been 100 psi. Most Wellingtons have their own compressor worked from a generator in the starboard engine to automatically top up the brake pressure. E-292 was one of the few Wellingtons that did not and should only have been used for cross-country flights where one landing was the norm. Before getting out of the aircraft to let us carry out the detail, Perry said to me 'you will be OK for the next circuit and landing and I will see to it that you get pressurised after that before carrying on'.

Once again we took off, the R/T still a garble. On the downwind leg I could see the lights of another Wellington making his approach to the runway but as I had ample space I carried on making my approach and landing. As our wheels touched I could see the white tail light of the other Wellington at the end of the runway but assumed he would turn off long before we got there (it is the No. 1 priority of any pilot to clear the runway as soon as possible). I touched my brakes as soon as the tail was down and the pressure dropped to fifteen pounds. At this point, halfway along the runway, I had passed the point where I could safely over-shoot, especially with another aircraft sitting on the end of it!

I applied full brakes and the pressure dropped to zero. I was now helpless with no brakes and therefore no steering. At this point I was running up quite fast on the other aircraft and judged that I would hit him slightly starboard, in which case my port propeller would chew up his rear gunner. On a Wellington it is only possible to stop one engine at a time. The cut out levers are in an awkward place to the rear and left of the pilot's seat. On my last 10 seconds before the crash I was pulling on the cut-out and the port engine was stopped as I hit the other Wellington. E-292 rode up the other Wellington's starboard wing with a horrible crunching noise, but no one got hurt.

At the Court of Inquiry I did not mention that P/O Perry had said it was all right to go off with so little brake pressure, and he did not mention it either! The pilot of the other aircraft did not know where to turn at the end of the runway and while having difficulty hearing the control R/T, had just sat there! (A few months later, poor Dobson and his crew were shot down on a Duisburg raid, there being no survivors. So his tail end Charlie only got another four months to live.)

In the RAF someone has to 'carry the can' regardless of mitigating circumstances. The upshot of it all was that my commission was stopped and my promotion to Flight Sergeant, which was automatically due, was put back for a year. I got no credit for saving the rear gunner's life. At least I was allowed to continue flying but I believe that everyone knew I got a raw deal.

* * * * *

The rest of the OTU course did not pass without incident either. On 7 June we were detailed for a 'Bullseye' exercise. This consisted of a long cross-country flight culminating with the dropping of practice bombs on the bombing range. A large number of Aircraft from OTUs and HCUs (Heavy Conversion Units for those crews intended for four-engined aircraft) were involved with proper target indicator flares on the range to simulate a real bombing operation.

We took off in Wellington K-3374 and climbed through scattered cloud on our first leg to Fishguard, South Wales. On our second leg to the Isle of Arran we observed that a few 'killer clouds' were building up. These clouds can reach from 800ft at their base to well over 30,000ft at the top, shaped like an anvil.

They are called Cumulus Nimbus and have extremely violent wind currents plus hail and lightning within.They have been responsible for the destruction of many aircraft. Our third leg was to Hull where we turned on to a southerly course heading towards the bombing range.

It was now dark and the cloud cover had built up to about 8/10ths so I decided to let down through the cloud to see the range. At 4,000ft I was still in cloud encountering extreme turbulence with hail battering the windscreen when suddenly the Wellington heaved up and was flung on its back. Now upside down, the compass toppled and the artificial horizon and altimeter also spun crazily round with the rest of the instrument needles flickering back and forth across their dials in rapid movement.

With all my instruments useless I was flying with the seat of my pants correcting the spin when we came out of the cloud at about 1,000ft. By the time I had levelled the wings and pulled the nose up we were only a few hundred feet above the ground.

Bob, the navigator, was the crew member who suffered most, as he had been pinned to the roof of his cabin with all his navigational instruments floating about him. He was always of a nervous disposition and this did not improve matters.

Stan the bomb-aimer soon established our position east of Sheffield from a distinct bend on the River Trent. We carried on and dropped our stick of practice bombs on the target and returned to base.

The only other time, in 15 years' flying, that I experienced a vicious Cu-Nim, was on 3 September 1948. I was piloting one of six Spitfires in formation from Dyce, Aberdeen to Linton-on-Ouse in Yorkshire, when on entering thick cloud we hit a Cu-Nim. Three of the Spitfires spun out of control. Our Squadron Leader, Joe Child, did not recover and crashed into the ground being killed instantly. F/Lt Gordon managed to pull out just missing the roof tops in the village of Ashington, in Northumberland, and F/Lt Innes pulled out at a couple of hundred feet. I felt much more comfortable in a Spitfire in those conditions but nevertheless I am certain that the 'killer cloud' we hit that night in the Wellington was by far the worst.

* * * * *

We returned to Finningley after a week's leave and were then posted to No. 1662 HCU, at Blyton near Gainsborough. There the crew was augmented by a flight engineer which brought us up to the heavy bomber complement of seven. The engineer's name was Gordon Leader, a Cumbrian from Workington. He was 10 years older than most of us and Tubby the rear gunner, who was the youngest, started calling him 'Dad'. That night we all went to the White Hart hotel in Gainsborough, and because our new crew member's favourite tipple was a black & tan we all had them, seven pints each.

The pace at Blyton that summer was at times frantic and this was perhaps reflected in the number of accidents involving a total of 11 Halifax bombers and the deaths of at least 40 men. The worst accident happened the day after we arrived when a Halifax crashed in flames near Wragby killing all eight men on board. Three days later, four more were killed and the other three badly injured when a Halifax came down on the Scunthorpe–Gainsborough road close to the airfield.

For four depressing days we ran about in our white vests and baggy blue shorts doing PT and other violent exercises. Then more ground school with engineering lectures pertaining to the Halifax 2s and 5s. Finally on the 19 July Don and I were airborne in the Halifax under the supervision of an instructor, F/Lt Kemp.

In addition to the greater power of its four Rolls-Royce Merlin engines the Halifax 5 was bigger, heavier, and less manoeuvrable and had more gadgets and instruments than any aircraft I had flown before. However, on the plus side it was stable in flight, spacious, had good visibility and on landing sat down on three points with a satisfying thud. Well perhaps not so satisfying for Don, for on my first landing I banged down so hard on the runway that standing on the few steps leading to the nose compartment, he collapsed down them with such a clatter I thought he must have broken his legs.

Over the next few weeks we carried out feathering drills and three engine flying and also cross-country flights and fighter affiliation exercises with the Spitfires from Digby.

On 29 July during a long cross-country flight, we were on a northerly heading crossing Wales when a piston in the port inner engine smashed through the crankcase and we had to feather it before it caught fire. The weather at base was low cloud and rain so we diverted to Mona, an airfield on the Isle of Anglesey.

On our next cross-country we were again diverted when the weather closed in at Blyton, this time to Seighford near Stafford. Our CO was not taking any chances because of the very heavy accident rate he was suffering.

Finally we finished the course and were posted to Lancaster Finishing School at Hemswell, Lincolnshire.

* * * * *

Much of what we were told about the Lancaster in ground school made little impression on me. My notebooks were filled with diagrams, graphs and formulae, but what I really learned was from my senses, from the sight, sound and feel of the aircraft.

The Lancaster looked good from every angle, strongly shaped and well proportioned. You boarded either through a door at the rear of the fuselage, starboard side or by climbing a ladder through the escape hatch into the nose. The pilot's seat was comfortable although fully raised it was still too low for me and I had to pad it up with anything at hand, usually on ops with bundles of Window. 'Window' was the code name for thin strips of metal foil dropped in bundles from aircraft which then appeared on enemy radar screens as 'false bombers'. It was the bomb-aimer's task to push Window through a chute near his right thigh.

All the crew were pleased with their stations, and none more than Stan the bomb-aimer, who had a panoramic view through his perspex blister in the nose. He lay on the padded door of the nose hatch to operate the bombsight and if he had to man the front turret, all he had to do was stand up and grab the triggers. Back over the hatch and up a step you came to the cabin, where the pilot and engineer sat side by side. Behind them the navigator sat facing to port in a little curtained office. Further aft was the wireless operator's compartment. His was the cosiest place in the aircraft, right next to the hot air outlet. He also had the astrodome above him, for the navigator's star shots, and the wireless-op., could keep a look out when he wasn't working his set. Still going aft, you would climb over the mass of the main spar then past the rest bed on the right into the long dark fuselage. After leaving the nose you would actually be walking on the roof of the bomb bay, but now you came to the end of that. You stepped down on to the fuselage floor and for the first time could stand upright, at least until you came to the mid-upper gun turret. You wriggled past the turret and felt your way on past the ammunition runways, then past the main door and the Elsan lavatory, to reach the rear turret entrance.

There was a list of things to do before you could start the engines, another list before moving out of dispersal and yet another before take-off. The last were the really important ones, and we called them VAs for vital actions. These differed slightly from one aircraft to another but for the Lancaster it was TMPFFGGH, trim, medium gear on the supercharger, pitch, fuel, flap, gills, gyro, hydraulics. The flight engineer made some of the checks himself such as checking the fuel gauges, that the master cocks and booster pumps were turned on and the cross feed turned off, selecting the right tank and then he followed me through on the rest.

However, the VAs were made at the marshalling point just before moving on to the runway for take-off. You had to get there from dispersal first, and this was the time that the Lancaster wasn't quite at her best. Having signalled to the ground crew to pull the chocks away from the main wheels, you then released the brakes and gave her a firm burst of power on all four engines to get her moving. You then had to negotiate a narrow winding perimeter track that might be more than a mile long, if you started from the upwind side of the airfield, to reach take-off point. You turned by gunning the outer engine on the side away from your turn, and straightened up by giving the opposite engine a burst, but there was a lot of inertia, and you had to anticipate each turn by 10 or 20 degrees depending on your speed. You were supposed to taxi at a fast walking pace but that wasn't easy to judge sitting 20ft above the ground. It was best to keep a good grip on the brake lever in case she ran away with you.

The first time I flew a Lancaster was on the 30 August 1944. F/Lt Rudge, a screen pilot sat beside me for the first few take-off and landings, with Don Leader standing vigilant behind him. After take-off Rudge instructed me to climb to 2,000ft where he stopped and feathered the two port engines and said 'do a 90 degree bank turn to port'. I did as instructed and was amazed that the Lancaster behaved as though all four engines were running. If I had done that in a Halifax 5 I would have dropped out of the sky. There I was standing on one wing tip, pulling hard round in a very tight turn, looking down at the ground through two dead engines. To say I was impressed would have been putting it mildly.

After that familiarisation flight we carried out four more details that same day which included the night flying check again with F/Lt Rudge, plus a further three and a half-hours solo night flying. We had been air-borne at 7.30am and touched down from our last detail at 11.15pm, a total of eight hours 20 minutes in the air. After just one day I felt as if I had been flying Lancasters for months.

It remained only to carry out three more short details in the Lancaster to bring us up to the required 12 hour total for the course. Then we awaited posting to a squadron.

It was a matter of pure chance which squadron topped the list for replacements. When our turn came we knew it would definitely be No. 1 Group and in Lincolnshire.

We had heard a lot of stories about casualties on the squadrons and how this or that crew we had trained with had 'got the chop'. Some squadrons were supposed to have better luck than others, better leadership or better maintenance. However, I felt confident of the Lancaster and my crew (with one exception) and paid little attention to the ominous stories.

Chapter 7
WICKENBY

On the afternoon of 11 September 1944 we and another crew whose Captain was F/O GT Bolderston, a Canadian, were taken by crew bus the short journey from Hemswell to Wickenby airfield, which lay 10 miles north east of Lincoln.

Wickenby is a name derived from the language of the Vikings who invaded and settled in Lincolnshire in the eighth century. *Wicken* means reeds or rushes (hence the English corruption, eg. wicker work, wicker basket, etc.) and *by* means place.The Vikings, therefore, knew Wickenby as the place by the reeds. As it can well be appreciated by those who have sojourned willingly or unwillingly in the flat, soggy fields of Bomber County, the name is more than appropriate.

RAF Wickenby was a purpose built bomber base constructed over the winter of 1942/43 and was the home of 12 Squadron and 626 Squadron of No. 1 Group, RAF Bomber Command. The airfield covered about 600 acres (2.4sq km) and had the usual three runway configuration with peripheral tracks, hard standings, a brick watchtower and numerous brick and metal buildings for the aircrews and ground staff. A number of buildings were to the east

(Communal Site, Living Quarters, WAAF Quarters) and stretched to and beyond the Lissington Road – a road travelled many an evening by the airmen and women who visited their favourite watering hole, the White Hart at Lissington. The Sick Quarters were to the south of the airfield together with another communal site and more living quarters.

Wickenby was first occupied in September 1942 by No. 12 Squadron (aircraft code PH) with 626 Squadron (a/c code UM) subsequently being formed in November 1943. 12 Squadron still exists to this day flying Tornado aircraft out of Lossiemouth. However, having spent its entire existence at Wickenby, 626 Squadron was disbanded on 14 October 1945.

Both Bolderston's crew and mine had been allocated to No. 626 Squadron and on reporting to the orderly room we were given forms which contained questions about next of kin, the disposal of personal articles and other enquiries that would help the administrative staff to deal with a dead man's belongings, estate and last wishes. The forms had to be completed there and then.

Our crew was then allocated sleeping quarters in a wooden hut about quarter a mile from the sergeants' mess. This we shared with half a dozen members of the Pioneer Corps who had labouring and driving duties in the bomb dump and elsewhere. They turned out to be great lads who kept the hut spick and span and the stove was always well supplied with fuel. We also had a few nights out with them in the village pub in Wragby which I think was called the Adam & Eve. These occasions entailed numerous pints of bitter, a singsong round the piano, then back in their lorry to our cosy hut where we had a supper of cocoa, toast and mushrooms.

The morning after our arrival we reported to the Flight Office and both Bolderston and myself were somewhat taken aback to find that we were on the battle order for operations that night as second pilots to F/O Thorpe and F/O Winder's crews respectively. I remember Bolderston's reaction; 'Bloody hell, I thought we would get at least a few days to settle in!' We were then welcomed to the squadron by the Flight Commander, Squadron Leader Shanley. I was then detailed for a fighter affiliation exercise in Lancaster Mk 3, R-Roger 2 with my own crew, after which I would be a member of F/O Winder's crew until after the operation.

I caught up with F/O Winder and his crew at Lancaster Y2's dispersal where they had completed their pre flight checks etc. It was about 2pm on a sunny afternoon and they were all relaxing on the grass verge of the concrete pan as I approached. The presence of a stranger disturbed most bomber crews, though all accepted the need for blooding new skippers. The jinx tag was strong; so many crews carrying 'second dickeys' were lost, that to the superstitious members of any crew it was an extra dread. I felt like the proverbial 'spare dick at a Jewish wedding'.

Winder gave me a perfunctory greeting with a raised hand and nodding towards the armourers, who were winching up the 4,000lb 'cookie' HE (high explosive) into the middle of the bomb bay, said 'We've got a fire load, that means the target will be a fairly large city'. I looked up into the bomb bay and saw that there were already 14 canisters of 4lb incendiaries in position. Each canister held 90 so there was a total of 1,260 incendiaries with a slightly later release and slower rate of fall, to land in the devastated area of the blockbuster.

We crowded into the curtained briefing room out of the afternoon sunlight and filed into our allotted row of chairs. All eyes stared at the red-ribboned route on the huge map above the platform culminating at the city of Frankfurt.

As the roll was called I watched the Station Commander settling into an armchair below the platform. He leafed through the papers on his table commenting on them in a whisper to the WAAF officer beside him. She was the junior intelligence officer and known to all as Clueless Kate. The Squadron Commander called for the intelligence briefing and the senior IO, blackboard pointer in one hand and pipe in the other, took his place.

'Well gentlemen, your target is Frankfurt, on the banks of the Main, here'. He jabbed the pointer at the map, where the river writhed through red-crayoned flak defences.

'Now, Frankfurt is, owing to its position, one of the most important German cities. It is an important railway centre and has a considerable trade along the river. Its position on the river…'

My attention wavered. I felt unable to concentrate, like in my schooldays, when I would gaze at the teacher, hearing but not listening, looking at the blackboard when he looked at it, smiling when he smiled. Like a mirror, seeing all, reflecting all, retaining nothing.

'...And in addition to its large industries it is encouraging the growth of firms specialising in light industries pertaining to the war effort. We hope that your visit tonight will do something to discourage that growth. The new war factories lie to the west of the city and tonight's attack...'

The met man, who had been preparing his slide projector at the back of the room, now crept to his seat in the front row stooping low as though fearful of obscuring, even for an instant, our view of the senior IO.

'...You form part of a force of 370 Lancasters from Nos. 1 and 3 groups. The pathfinder force technique is on the board here...' The senior IO descended from the platform and approached the blackboard, pointer at the ready.

'Here is your target. This is your last leg into the target, a narrow turn to port when your bombs have gone, and your route out. You are primarily to bomb the red target indicators shown by these red blobs. If no red TIs are visible then bomb the centre of the cluster of green backers up. If cloud conditions prohibit the use of ground marking methods the sky marking will be by red flares dripping green stars.'

He tapped the appropriate illustration with his pointer and got back on to the platform.

'Right, now, as to defences, the main opposition will be barrage flak on the run in to the target and over it. You can also expect heavy searchlight activity. If you are coned, try and dive out of it quickly as the flak will be accurate and will be bursting 17 seconds after the searchlights lock on. Now, if anyone has the misfortune to be forced down in the target area, the best bet would be to make for the French frontier north of Strasbourg. This part of the frontier is still not heavily guarded, and if you can reach this area on the map under cover of darkness...'

We had heard that crews who baled out over the target and descended into the city streets were liable to be summarily dispatched by the more vengeful citizens – by hanging on a lamp post or by combustion on the nearest fire.

'Don't forget to empty your pockets before you go and, Captains, check that each of your crew has his escape aids and money wallet before you leave the briefing room.' The Squadron Commander did not waste words: 'Right Met.'

The met man hastily mounted the platform and lowered a white screen over the wall map by manipulating a system of cords and pulleys. The lights were put out and the voice of the met man rose above the hum of the projector. 'This is the estimated synoptic situation for 23:00 hrs tonight. Base conditions for take-off will be good, also very little cloud on route and practically no cloud over the target itself. Base conditions on return…'

The met man ended his briefing with surprising theatricality by stepping into his projector's beam and bowing stiffly towards the CO.

'Right Navigation.'

The nav leader stepped up; he was F/Lt Len Allison*, a gangling officer with a sallow complexion and a very battered peak cap. 'Have all the navigators got their flimsies? Right, I'll run through the set course and turning points for the first wave. Second wave people…' I thought, he looks like a good navigator to have in one's crew. I was to find out how wrong I was. 'Right check your watches. It is coming up to 14 minutes past four – 10 seconds to go – five seconds – four – three – two – one – now; 16:14.'

The next to speak was the bombing leader, a lanky Canadian, who read quietly from his notes without embellishment or gesture. He told of jettison bars, terminal velocities and photoflashes, but the dry manner of his speech set my mind wandering again. It occurred to me that notwithstanding all the expensive training lavished on me, no one had informed me the duties of a second pilot. I knew that they would have little to do with the success of the operation because there was but one set of controls in the Lancaster. I deduced that I would take over some of the engineer's duties; after all I was depriving him of his seat.

The signals leader, who appeared anxious to draw as little attention to himself as possible, addressed the audience diffidently. 'I should like to see all the wireless operators after the briefing.'

The gunnery leader then got up. He was a short stocky Englishman with fair hair and moustache, hands in pocket, cap at an angle. 'Remember that you

* Not his real name.

gunners are responsible for the safety of the crew from enemy attack the entire time you are in the air. Keep your eyes peeled. Don't narrow your search to one quarter. Swing your turrets round and keep your eyes moving all the time. Watch especially for attacks from underneath. Captains can help their gunners here by dipping a wing at regular intervals so that the mid-upper gunner can search directly underneath. If you are attacked be prompt and lucid with your evasive action and keep your Captain informed at all times just where the fighter is. As he moves around you pass him on to whoever is in the best position to watch him. Don't waste ammunition on him while he is out of range but give him everything you've got if he comes in close.' He took his hands out of his pockets and turned towards the Station Commander. 'That's all sir.'

The man from Flying Control, a good looking bloke supposedly an actor in peacetime, began with instructions about taxiing and a description of the perimeter lighting. He then spoke of the runway.

'From what met said it seems we shall be able to use the long runway for take-off and the wind should be light enough for us to use it all night although you might have a slight cross-wind when you get back. If the wind speed warrants a change of runway we will let you know on the R/T when you rejoin the circuit. I don't need to impress on you the need for strict R/T silence before take-off. Leave your sets on stud 'A', base frequency, in case there's an urgent message for you. Join the circuit on return at 2,000ft, call control and let us know you are back. We will give you a height to circle at, then we will bring you down in 500ft steps until it's your turn to land. Acknowledge each instruction so we know that you are not flying up someone else's tail. When you get 'prepare to land', come down to 1,000ft, switch your downward identification light on and position yourself a reasonable distance behind the aircraft on 'pancake'. Let us know when you are downwind. The aircraft in front of you should be down and close to clearing the runway when you come round to the funnel lights, lined up for landing. Call again there – just say your aircraft letter and 'funnels'. We will either say 'pancake', or 'continue approach', or 'go round again'. When you are down, taxi clear of the runway as soon as you can and call 'clear'.'

There was a ripple of movement over the room as the Station Commander, Group Captain Haynes, stood up. He cocked an eyebrow at the map. 'There's nothing I wish to add to what you already know. Your meal was ordered for five o'clock, it's five past now, so you'd better hurry. Locker rooms at five-thirty. Good luck.'

* * * * *

After a hurried meal we prepared ourselves for flight and then the crew bus took us to Y 2's dispersal where we climbed aboard.

The day had been fine and bright and the sun was just above the horizon as we took off. We climbed in a circle over Wickenby and levelling off at 2,000ft set course for Reading. I did not like sitting on a jump seat on the right hand side as this was not nearly as comfortable as the pilot's seat.

At Reading we altered course for Beachy Head and crossing the English Channel dropped altitude to 1,000ft to avoid being picked up by the German long-range radar. Thundering over France, our route took us over the World War One battle areas – Arras, St Quentin and Verdun and after passing Nancy we started our climb into Germany. It was now quite dark and just before reaching our last turning point over the Rhine a massive explosion occurred ahead of us in the Black Forest, south west of Karlsruhe. Winder said, 'two Lancs have collided'. We reached the turning point over the burning remains of the Lancasters and turned on to our heading for Frankfurt, still climbing.

We were now at our bombing height of 17,000ft and many searchlight beams were waving ahead. Skirting Mannheim on our port side a Lancaster was picked up by the blue tinged master beam. Immediately about seven other beams swung on to him and I watched fascinated as the pinpoint flashes of flak burst all around him. He was quite a distance away but I could see that he was taking furious evasive action. Despite this the cone followed him through it all until eventually he caught fire and plunged to earth. A few minutes later another Lancaster was coned but instead of going down in flames he exploded with a huge orange flash.

Nearing Frankfurt I stared at the sky in front of us. Among the groping searchlight beams the white and yellow flak bursts formed a sparkling wall. It was hard to believe that we could pass through that unceasing barrage. Was it always like this? I looked at Winder. He appeared unexcited, slumped in his seat, hands resting loosely on the control wheel. He didn't appear to acknowledge the bomb-aimer's sing song chant of guidance:

'Steady…steady…tracking in nicely, steady…bomb doors open.' Winder opened the doors, still without comment, but we could feel the drag and extra buffeting as they opened.

'Steady…left, left…steady.'

The flickering wall ahead was now to our right, to our left, above us and below. Parallel lines of tracer bullets made an intermittent winking curve through the darkness. I saw another bomber, exhausts glowing orange, drift across our flight path. I looked down on Frankfurt through the engineer's blister. Shimmering pulses of light showed the city below as the 4,000lb cookies hit the ground. The river gleamed, darkened, and gleamed again.

The bombs dropped. Winder swung the wheel to port as the bomb doors closed. Gradually the searchlights and the barrage fell behind us. A sense of relief came over me.

Our return route was more direct and we only took two hours and 40 minutes to base, compared with the four hours and 50 minutes from base to the target. A total of seven hours 30 minutes in the air.

Twenty-three Lancasters failed to return from the night's operation. Two were missing from our Squadron – F/O Collens and F/Lt Thorpe. We were told later that all of Thorpe's crew including F/O Bolderston their 'second dickey' had been killed. However, on carrying out research for this book I discovered from Squadron 626 records that in fact six of them including Thorpe and Bolderstone baled out successfully after being shot down by a night fighter. Tragically, however, Bolderston and two others are reported as having then been murdered by German civilians whereas mercifully F/Lt Dennis Thorpe and another two crew members were captured and interned in Stalags 1 and 7 respectively.

Chapter 8

THE CREW'S FIRST OPERATION

By the time I had attended de-briefing after the Frankfurt raid and had operational breakfast, it was after 3am when I got back to the hut. As I entered, the crew gathered round me and asked in unison, 'How was it Jock?' I gave them an account of the raid as I saw it and informed them that two of the squadron's Lancasters were missing including the one Bolderston was on.

I had been particularly watching our navigator Bob Grey's reaction. The whole crew knew of his nervousness. During our training whenever I indulged in low flying he always got agitated and asked me to stop. On one of our last details at the Lancaster finishing school, Don and I had stopped and feathered three of the engines. The rest of the crew trusted us but Bob was in a state of panic. His navigational skills were adequate in normal conditions, but would they break down if he were cowering in a blue funk during an operation? Our problem was soon to be dramatically resolved.

As there were no operations on for tonight, we were detailed for a night cross-country exercise in Lancaster X-Ray 2. We took off at 7.30pm and climbed away on the first leg. After we reached an altitude of 15,000ft, Bob complained that he was suffering severe stomach pains. I said, 'you will be all right Bob once you have a good fart,' but Stan reported to me that Bob was rolling about on the floor of his cubicle, obviously in agony. I informed the crew that we would be returning to base, turned on to a homing course and started losing altitude.

Later, on asking Bob how he was feeling, he said that his pains gradually left him as we descended. I told him he must report to the Station Medical Officer next morning.

While Bob was undergoing extensive medical and decompression tests, we flew fighter affiliation and air gunnery exercises without him.

The following day the Flight Commander and myself were called to a meeting with the Station MO. He bluntly told us that he was categorising Bob Grey as LMF. It seems that he had feigned severe stomach pains when he thought he was at 15,000ft in the decompression tank, when in fact he was still at ground level.

Bob was posted that same day. After packing his kit bag he sorrowfully shook hands with us and departed. We never did hear what happened to him after that.

It was not until three or four years after the war that pieces about the psychological strain of flying a tour of operations began to appear in newspapers and learned periodicals. Dr David Stafford-Clark in the *Journal of Medical Science* said that on a tour of 30 operations a man's morale, starting at high, rose slightly at first because of the excitement but then steadily declined going close to crack-up level at about the 12th operation. When the 13th operation had been passed, morale rose very slightly until about the 22nd sortie when it dipped, and continued to dip towards the crack-up level. Dr Stafford-Clark pointed out in his report that men who had joined simply for the glamour of being RAF aircrew usually cracked up fairly quickly. In Bob's case that was even before the first hurdle!

All aircrew were volunteers. No man was ever ordered to climb into an aeroplane and fly over enemy territory. Every last one of us had applied to fly and, if we had not applied, we would not have been flying.

To that extent we were masters of our own destiny, and after each 30 trips, any flyer could opt for a breather…but always with the proviso that, in time, he would be back operational flying again.

Needless to say you could always be invalided out of flying duties – 'catch a packet' and you were out. But volunteering out of aircrew part way through a tour – and volunteering out forever – was a different matter altogether. Theoretically it was possible, even ostensibly as straightforward as the original volunteering, but…

That 'but' represented those three letters LMF. If you sent in a request to be taken off flying duties then you put your whole future at risk. Not merely your future in the RAF, but your future for the rest of your life. The request would be opposed but, if you dug your heels in, it would be granted. However, unless you had a damn good reason, every document concerning your RAF career would be stamped large with those damning letters – LMF 'Lacking in Moral Fibre'.

Ask any man in Bomber Command who completed a tour of operations, and he will disapprove of a man having been given the LMF label after doing 18, perhaps 20 ops or more. Going through a heavily defended German target in a bomber in World War Two has been likened to 'going over the top' in the First. For a man to have gone 'over the top' even only three or four times and then refused, and for him to be then considered lower than the low, only fit for latrine duties and things like that, seems to me to be terribly unjust.

However, if our navigator was one who should never have survived the aircrew selection process, our crew had little sympathy for him at that time. As a crew we would have to fly with odd-bod navigators for the immediate future at any rate. However, eventually fortune was to smile on us.

* * * * *

On our return from a week's leave, there was no spare navigator available. I asked Stan if he would take over as navigator as there seemed to be plenty of spare bomb-aimers. I would have had no qualms about Stan taking over. He had a nimble adaptable mind, was conscientious, cool in an emergency and was proficient with the complex navigational aids carried in the Lancaster. After much thought, however, he declined and I did not press him further.

Accordingly we now looked to the Navigation Leader for assistance. Normally he would have already done a tour of operations but was allowed to do two or three extra trips per month if the situation allowed.

On 5 October therefore we were briefed for a night raid on Saarbrucken with Nav., leader F/Lt Allison as our navigator. The target city was situated right on the Siegfried Line close to the French border and as I later learned, the raid was made at the request of the American Third Army which was advancing in this direction. The intention was to cut the railways and block supply routes generally through the town.

We took off before dusk and Len Allison gave me a course for Reading. After about five minutes I was somewhat surprised when he poked his head out of the curtain and asked, ' Where's the stream Jock?' I replied that it was about eight miles port of us and he said I had better turn port 15 degrees. It was now getting dark although I could see we were passing through the main stream of bombers but said nothing. After a while Len again asked me where the stream now was. I told him it was now about five miles starboard and he said, 'Mmm, better turn 10 degrees starboard, no make it five'.

I was puzzled and asked Len if his Gee Box had packed in. He said no. Gee was the code name for a radio pulse system by which the navigator could fix his position by reference to three transmitting stations in England. It was extremely quick and accurate compared with the now outdated astro-navigation. It had a range of nearly 400 miles but was usually jammed by the Germans at the extreme ranges. However, over and up to a range of 100 miles from England, there was no problem and it was a navigator's dream, providing he kept up a good air-plot on the navigation chart.

In furtherance, it was a group requirement to calculate a 'wind' and check the ground speed every 10 minutes while Gee lasted. In practical terms this meant continuous work, particularly at the outset, with pencil, ruler, protractor and dividers. Gradually, with the help of Gee and the Dalton computer, the wind pattern for the night emerged so that later, when radar faded, the navigator had reasonable data on which to base his dead reckoning.

It was now dark and the bomber stream had disappeared from view. I suspected it was now away ahead of us. When I asked Len if he wanted me to increase the speed, he said, 'Yes please!!'

Even with increased speed our heavily laden bomber made little impression on the gap, and as zero hour approached we were a long, long way from the target.

On a compact target like Saarbrucken the timing was crucial. There were only two waves. The first wave bombed from zero hour which was 10.30pm to six minutes after zero hour. The second wave was from six minutes to 12 minutes after.

So by 10.42pm there shouldn't have been any bombers over the target, and by all accounts there weren't. However, 15 miles away a lone Lancaster was stooging towards Saarbrucken; R. Roger 2 with its sprog crew on their first raid, but with an experienced navigator!

Thankfully, apart from Len, only Stan and I were aware of the extreme danger we were in.

The guns had stopped firing and the target indicators were all out as we approached. Many fires were burning and Stan bombed the centre of those which appeared to be the main town area, north of the River Saar, through which the railway lines ran. After the bombs had gone, the guns opened up and we had their undivided attention. I rammed the throttles forward and stuffed the nose down, at the same time turning starboard onto a homeward heading.

Shells were bursting on our port and if I had left the turn any later we would have been right in the middle of them. I kept zigzagging until well clear of the target before steadying on to a westerly course.

In retrospect, I can only assume that our luck in getting away from that situation was owing to the following factors: we were too late to be classed as a straggler and any German fighters would have left before we arrived. Also, it was not a heavily defended area like the Ruhr otherwise the crack German anti-aircraft batteries at such a location would have made short work of us.

As regards the poor navigation, I think Len was trying to save himself a lot of work by lining up with the bomber stream and working out from that the true wind which the other navigators had worked out. However, early darkness and a drastic change of wind from that which was forecast foiled him.

Any other navigator, apart from the navigation leader, would have got a large flea in his ear if he had submitted a chart which was obviously devoid of the navigational work required.

Crossing the French coast on our return, Greg received a message from Group diverting us to Methwold in Norfolk, as Lincolnshire was shrouded in fog.

After landing, Len offered no apology or explanation for his poor performance. I preferred to think that he was ashamed of his laziness and not that he was disdainful of my relatively low rank of Sergeant.

* * * * *

Once the fog had cleared we returned to Wickenby just after noon. Soon after 6pm, operations were ordered for the following morning and we were again on the battle order, with Len Allison as our navigator.

At the 8.30am briefing on 8th October, 1 Group was detailed to bomb Emmerich and 3 & 4 Groups to bomb Kleve. These two small German towns, which lay close to the Dutch border, stood on the approach routes by which German units could threaten the vulnerable Allied right flank near Nijmegen, which had been left exposed by the failure of Operation 'Market Garden'.

R. Roger 2 was again allocated and we took off at 11.30am. Len gave me an initial course of 120 degrees and soon started the same caper as at Saarbrucken… 'Where is the stream Jock? Oh well, let me see, alter course 15 port, no, make it 10.' Stan poked his head up from the nose compartment, looked at me, shook his head and rolled his eyes upward. We crossed and re-crossed the bomber stream until eventually our course coincided with theirs.

The scattered cloud below had cleared as we crossed the Dutch coast at the Hague. Tracking between Arnhem and Nijmegen at our bombing altitude of

10,000ft, the targets showed up clearly on either side of the Rhine. Huge columns of smoke billowed up from Kleve, which 3 & 4 Groups had hit first.

On the bombing run into Emmerich the three waves seemed to be bunched up into one long second wave. The flak was not too heavy but it was extremely accurate. Ahead of us three Lancasters were hit in quick succession. The first was just a massive explosion and he must have been hit in his bomb load. The other two went down in flames and we counted five parachutes from one Lancaster and four from the other.

Stan dropped our load on a red target indicator dripping over Emmerich, which was now almost completely obscured by smoke. As I then turned south on to a westerly heading, I could see clearly the first five parachutes drifting in to the billowing smoke and fires of Kleve. The other four parachutes landed on the banks of the Rhine between the two towns.

I wondered what would become of them. Ominous reports had been filtering out of Germany to our intelligence people that the enraged German populace was putting more and more members of bomber crews to death. Captains of bombers were now allowed to draw revolvers and ammunition from the armoury stores. It was thought that a firearm might be able to hold a lynch mob at bay until the German army or the police could take you into custody for transfer to a prison camp.

We landed at 4.30pm it having been a short five-hour trip. Next day I signed for a 38 Smith & Wesson revolver and 24 bullets.

Fortunately I never had cause to use my Smith & Wesson. It would probably have been futile in any case as if I had used this on a German police officer or civilian I reckon I would have needed the last bullet for myself.

Whether a member of a bomber crew survived or not after bailing out was just down to chance and this was illustrated by poor F/O Bolderston's fate when contrasted with the amazing story of Arthur Lee, a navigator with 626 Squadron who I became friendly with after the war.

In January 1944 the battle of Berlin was at its height. Between November 1943 and March 1944 the entire strength of Bomber Command was hurled against the 'Big City' and 16 major attacks were carried out on the German capital. For most of this period the weather was atrocious and few crews ever saw the city beneath the clouds. The Luftwaffe in turn deployed all their night fighters to combat the threat and these were at the peak of their efficiency. Bomber Command lost 300 aircraft in the battle which represented a loss rate of 6.4 per cent. Bombers from Wickenby took part in every attack and suffered its fair share of the heavy losses.

On the night of 27/28th January, Wickenby lost four aircraft in yet another 'maximum effort'. Three of these were from 12 squadron and the other, Lancaster Sugar 2 from 626 Squadron, was captained by an Australian Flight Lieutenant Bill Balford with Arthur as his navigator. Bill was on his eighth raid on Berlin and after leaving Wickenby at dusk, and helped by a strong tail wind, he arrived over Berlin some two and a half hours later. Following a blind attack through cloud in which they aimed at the flares dropped by the Pathfinders, Bill swung Sugar 2 south for the Czechoslovakian border. He then turned west into the headwind to make painfully slow progress towards the Rhine and beyond that hopefully safety. However, just before 11pm, when Sugar 2 was some 20 miles short of the Rhine and 10 miles south of track, it was brought down by the cannon fire of a stalking ME 110. It fell from 23,000ft in a blazing spiral dive.

On the ground Rudi Balzer watched its fall and saw an engine drop from the wing followed by a mid-air explosion. As the flaming wreckage crashed into a wood on the high ground beyond his village he then saw, by the glare of the burning aircraft, a single parachute descending.

Rudi was a soldier in the German army, on leave at the time from the Eastern Front in his home village of Katzenelnbogen some 20 miles south east of Koblenz in the beautiful hill country known as the Taunus. It has a history going back thousands of years and boasts an ancient castle. After seeing the parachute come down he took his father's motorcycle and drove to the site of the crash. There he found Arthur Lee who had been tied to a tree by local inhabitants. Seeing that Arthur was suffering from cuts and burns he took charge of the situation, released him and took him to his own family doctor for treatment. While they were there a local policeman arrived and implied that they were taking Arthur to be lynched – there was an angry crowd outside calling for vengeance on the English *Terrorflieger.* Rudi countered that the Englishman was a prisoner of war and under his protection. The policeman made a move to pull his pistol but Rudi was quicker on the draw with his own gun and the policeman then thought better of it. Rudi took Arthur to the Burgomaster's office and was present when the leader of the local Nazi party ordered the Burgomaster to shoot Arthur. Again Rudi insisted that the airman was under his protection, adding that he would not hesitate to use his pistol if anyone tried to infringe that protection. He remained with his prisoner all night and into the following day until a Luftwaffe truck came and took Arthur away into legal captivity.

Arthur was of course extremely fortunate to have Rudi Balzer as his protector. As a soldier in the Wermacht he refused to obey any orders which conflicted with the requirements of the Geneva Convention. More crucially, as a compassionate human being, he gave protection and kindness to another human being in peril. After being fed, one kindness which Arthur never forgot was when Rudi folded the parachute to make a makeshift mattress on the floor of the Burgomaster's office and covered him with his army greatcoat.

These were two young men, both 22 years old, caught up in events not of their making, on opposing sides in a brutal and savage war. Rudi had to show that he was ready to use force to protect his prisoner even if it meant incurring the wrath of his superiors. As he said to Arthur later: 'We were both in great danger – you were to be shot and I was to be court martialled.'

Arthur hadn't fully comprehended the danger he was in at the time. He understood no German and only remembered that there was lots of shouting and arguing and that 'they all seemed to be very upset about something'. However, he never forgot the kindness of 'that young German soldier' and after the war he tried to trace him without success. That is until a reunion was held in 1982 for 12 and 626 squadrons at the Post House Hotel in Leicester which Arthur and I both attended. It turned out that the manager of the Post House, Hans Gemmer, would you believe it, was born in Katzenelnbogen! After further careful enquiries and research Arthur finally met Rudi again after

40 years in Katzenelnbogen on 13 October 1984. Following that, they and their families met several times both in England and Germany until Arthur died on 22 October 1986 from a heart attack. Rudi Balzer died on 7 February 2000 after a long illness bravely borne.

While chatting to Arthur at a reunion he told me why he thought he was the only survivor, although he was certain he was the last to leave the stricken aircraft. On the night before that fateful trip they had also been briefed to go to Berlin and were sitting in the aircraft ready to go when the flares went up from the tower and the operation was scrubbed, probably because of the weather. He remembered that they leapt aboard the crew bus for the ride back to their quarters but that none of them took their parachutes. The chutes therefore remained in the aircraft all night which was a very wet and cold one.

The next day, Thursday 27 January had dawned bright and clear and ops were on again. The ribbon on the briefing room map again displayed the route to Berlin and Arthur's crew cycled to the distant aircraft dispersal for the pre-flight checks. The parachutes were there where they had left them but Arthur thought his was damp and with a strong instinct for self preservation, decided to change it. The others, however, decided that for them this would be an unnecessary chore which would involve a long ride around the perimeter track back to the parachute store.

Arthur concluded to me: 'My six friends died that night. Were their parachutes damp? Did they freeze solid at 20,000ft?' Their bodies were found close to the wreckage of the burnt out aircraft and a later report noted that some of the parachutes had been partially deployed.

Arthur's six fellow crew members are buried in Rheinberg war cemetery. He was interned for the duration of the war in Camp L6/357. This same crew had survived a ditching in the North Sea following a raid on Stettin just three weeks before on 5–6 January. They had been airborne for over 10 hours and their Lancaster was completely out of petrol when they came down approximately 100 miles off Withernsea on the Yorkshire coast. All were rescued and there were no injuries. Their reprieve was to prove tragically short lived.

Chapter 9

OPERATION HURRICANE

By the beginning of October the Allied drive across France had been halted. The battle lines had hardened west of the river Meuse and Bomber Command, which had been temporarily tied up with military commitments, was about to resume a full offensive against large industrial areas in Germany.

On 13 October 1944, Sir Arthur Harris (known affectionately to the public as 'Bomber' Harris and less affectionately to aircrews as 'Butcher' or 'Butch') received the directive for operation 'Hurricane' – 'In order to demonstrate to the enemy in Germany generally the overwhelming superiority of the Allied air forces in this theatre…the intention is to apply within the shortest practical period the maximum effort of the Royal Air Force Bomber Command and the VIIIth United States Bomber Command against objectives in the densely populated Ruhr'.

It seems that Bomber Command had been forewarned of the directive because a battle order was posted on the Squadron notice board on Friday 13 October with our names, again with Len Allison as navigator. We retired early to our sleeping quarters knowing that we would be called early.

The call came at two in the morning, and after breakfast we trooped into the briefing room. The senior Intelligence Officer opened the proceedings. He informed us that today's operation against Duisburg would be the greatest daylight raid ever on a German city. Over a thousand bomber aircraft would take part in an assault lasting half an hour.

Duisburg was at that time the largest river port in Europe. It produced heavy machinery and its docks and railway marshalling yards were vital communication centres. The attack would be controlled by a Master Bomber code-named 'Bigboy' who would instruct the bomber stream, code-named 'Thunder', as to aiming points over the radio transmission. The stream would fly at between 16,000ft and 20,000ft and be covered by Spitfires and Mustangs flying at between 30,000ft and 35,000ft.

The Met Officer then took the stage and predicted that the blanket of cloud, which at present extended over England and Northern France, would disperse before the stream reached the German border leaving good visibility over the target area. Our Len then got up and gave his usual crisp, efficient briefing, finishing with the synchronising of watches. The bombing, signals and gunnery leaders followed him, each speaking a few words and briefing was concluded by the Commanding Officer wishing all crews good luck.

We collected parachutes and at 5am, buses began to transport the crews to their aircraft which stood at single dispersal points round the perimeter of the airfield. At our Roger 2's dispersal it was still dark as we joked with the ground crew and then climbed aboard. At least I had the comforting thought that dawn would soon be with us. I preferred daylight operations.

On the test runs on the engines Don and I encountered magneto drops on the two port engines but I decided to go. All checks were now completed and I taxied out and joined the queue of Lancasters from the two squadrons slowly moving round to the take-off point. At 6.31am Roger 2 got a green from the caravan and was ready for take-off.

I opened the throttles while Don watched the boost and rev needles swing round. He especially eyed the boost gauges as they generally gave the first sign of engine trouble. With all engines pulling Don took over the throttles when three-quarters open, pushed them to, then through the gate, the gauges showing 3,000rpm, speed approaching 90kts. At 95kts I could feel the wheels unstick and selected undercarriage up, also taking up the flaps five degrees at a time.

At 155kts I started a climbing turn to port and was soon in cloud. At 8,000ft we broke through the cloud to see a clear blue sky and Len gave me a course for the first turning point at Reading. There were lots of bombers surrounding us and I could see more of them bursting through the cloud below.

The forecast wind must have been accurate, as I could see as the bomber stream formed that we were right in the middle of it and stayed there.

The cloud was beginning to break up as we crossed the Dutch coast and Stan reported that we were passing Rotterdam on our port. We flew on in the security of the stream and on approaching the Ruhr I noticed that aircraft in the distance ahead were wheeling on to a new course. They had bombed and were leaving the target. Roger 2 cruised on with puffs of smoke from flak bursts visible, tight black balls with a flashing centre that, as they dispersed, expanded and looked even worse.

Then we heard the Master Bomber's voice, ' Bigboy to Thunder, Freehand', which was the code word for pick your own target. I assumed that because there was still a lot of cloud below, the MB was in a dilemma whether to employ ground or sky marking and just chose the easiest way out.

Stan asked for bomb doors opened. Flak was exploding on either side. I looked down through a gap in the clouds and saw a thread of silver, beyond which spread the dark stain of an extensively built up city. To the right, clouds of black smoke were billowing up but Stan had spotted a huge built up area through a gap in the clouds and directed me, ' Right, right, steady, steady – bombs away, bomb doors closed'. I gave it a few seconds to allow the camera a shot before banking hard port to follow the rest of the stream.

Back at base, two and half-hours later, we were transported to the briefing room. At most bomber stations after a raid, aircrews were offered a good measure of rum as well as their coffee. Unfortunately, Wickenby was not one of them. I sure could have done with a glass of demerara when we were informed that we were on ops again that night as soon as the aircraft were refuelled and bombed up. We felt cheated, not having any leisure before being pitched without respite on another raid.

* * * * *

No one slept during the afternoon and after an early supper we reported for briefing. It was a surprise to learn that the target was Duisburg again.

Before briefing commenced, Squadron Leader Shanley, our Flight Commander, had taken me aside and introduced me to Pilot Officer Marbaix who was to be our navigator for that night's mission. P/O Marbaix had just arrived on our squadron with his crew. He had completed 19 ops in a previous tour but his Captain, F/O Charland, a Canadian, was inexperienced and was to fly as second pilot in F/O Campbell's crew who had completed over 20 sorties.

We were assured that the morning's raid had been a tremendous success and that – only! – 13 Lancasters and one Halifax had been shot down. Tonight's raid, another thousand plus bomber effort, would wipe out what was left of Duisburg off the map. Twenty Mosquitos dropping Window would carry out a diversionary raid on Hamburg and this, with luck, should draw off the enemy night fighters.

This was the first time that two separate thousand-bomber raids had been mounted in such quick succession and the ground crews were sorely pressed. Our own Lancaster, Roger 2 had been taken out of service to get four new engines and we had been allotted O – Oboe 2. When we arrived at dispersal, refuelling had just been completed but bombing up had just started.

Now approaching 10pm, we were beginning to feel the effects of the long day as we watched, dispassionately, our navigator chivvying the armourers to speed up their task of loading 12 1,000lb bombs into Oboe's bomb bay. Gus Marbaix was anxious to get started with his second tour and did not want us to miss the take-off deadline. We did not feel like it then, but were to thank our lucky stars that this keen so-and-so had been detailed as our navigator this night.

Three of the squadron's Lancasters failed to get off before the deadline but Oboe 2 was first off, entirely due to Gus's prodding. It was a dark night and no other bombers could be seen as I turned on to the first course to Reading although I could certainly feel their slipstreams. To foil the enemy radar system the stream would fly at 1,000ft most of the way across France and then climb to 18,000ft before reaching the battle lines.

There were four legs to the target and four legs back, but long before the target I knew we had a good navigator. His crisp requests for courses and speeds gave me the feeling that here was a man on top of his job. Mind you, courses and speeds had to be accurately adhered to by the pilot and the navigator had repeats of the altimeter, airspeed indicator and compass facing him, so he could easily assess the pilot's reliability.

Here I would like to pay tribute to our Boffins who produced the MkIII Automatic Pilot. During my training in America I had used the 'Sperry' autopilot when flying Catalina flying boats over the Gulf of Mexico. This was reputed to be the best in the world but was bulky and expensive. The MkIII was produced at a fraction of the cost of a Sperry and took up less than half the space. Providing that the aircraft was properly trimmed before engagement, it could control an aircraft with much greater accuracy than a human pilot. For example, it could hold a course without going more than one degree off either side. Vacuum motors powered it and the proviso was that it had to be disengaged at least half an hour before the target because the bombsight also used vacuum motors for its gyros and needed all the vacuum pump's capacity.

There had been a few instances of heavy bombers diving into the ground and the autopilot had been blamed but it had never been proved conclusively. A lot of pilots never used it over Germany because they weaved all the time hoping to foil night fighters attacking from underneath. Whenever Frank, the mid-upper gunner, wanted to look below the aircraft it was an instantaneous action for me to flick out 'George' (the nickname for the autopilot) and roll the Lancaster either to port or starboard. Needless to say, being a lazy person, 'George' did most of the flying and I got all the credit.

Gus had navigated us dead on track and time, and the target appeared ahead. A Ruhr target was always heavily defended and this one was no exception. The target indicators were dropping beautiful blooms of red and green flares but above them there was a deadly sparkle of unleashed flak. Stan then took over, 'Bomb doors open, left, left, steady, steady, bombs away'. The Lancaster lurched upwards as over five tons of bombs left its belly.

The bomb doors had hardly closed when a searchlight swung on to us. The cockpit was as bright as day. I turned sharply to port and dived steeply. I had seen the deadly result of being coned during the Frankfurt raid and was desperate to avoid that. Our speed was now over 300mph as I pulled hard starboard and left the beam behind. We had lost over 2,000ft but were now in welcome darkness. Gus gave me a course of 285 to steer as we regained lost altitude.

Oboe's wheels touched down at base just after 4am. At the debriefing Gus kept looking round for his Skipper but ominously, all the other squadron Lancasters landed except for the one flown by F/O Campbell.

By the time we had breakfast and got back to our hut we had been 28 hours without sleep and had been in the air for more than 10 and a half-hours.

Later that day it was confirmed that F/O Campbell and crew along with Gus Marbaix's pilot, F/O Charland, had all been killed over Duisburg. Rather than return to OTU with his headless crew, Gus asked me if he could stay as our navigator. I felt like jumping in the air and shouting 'Yippee!', but constrained myself to, 'We'd be delighted to have you Gus'. We approached Wing Commander John Molesworth, the Squadron Commander, and it was settled.

* * * * *

For the next few days bad weather restricted operations. An amusing story filtered down from Group Headquarters concerning Winston Churchill. Seemingly he had written to Met Office HQ complaining of the poor forecasting affecting the RAF bombing raids into Germany. The Met Office replied that they got 40 per cent of their forecasts correct, which under the circumstances of that time, they considered a good effort. Churchill replied: 'In that case, if we had acted upon the opposite of your forecasts, we would have got it 60 per cent right.'

On 19 October we were briefed for an attack on Stuttgart, lying about 50 miles south east of Mannheim. We were to be in a small force of Lancasters with a zero hour of 8.30pm while a much larger force would attack later at 1am.

We took off in P – Peter 2 late in the afternoon and flew over England in the gathering dusk. It was going to be a tricky navigational sortie. The weather was bad and visual pinpoints were unobtainable. On top of that our Gee box had gone on the blink. Gus asked Stan's assistance in working the H2S set which was a radar device. A scanner under the aircraft's belly sent pulses earthwards and these were refracted back to a small screen when they hit a built up area. A good operator could also pick up large rivers and coastlines. Unfortunately, the Germans had previously retrieved a set from a crashed bomber and their night fighters could now home on to the transmissions and therefore over Germany you used it at your peril. I could hear on the intercom that Stan was reading the screen well and was contributing significantly to Gus's navigation.

Half an hour before zero hour Stan went forward to his bombing position. Pathfinder Mosquitos would be dropping red TIs at zero hour. There were many cloud layers at different levels and we could easily miss seeing the TIs if we were far off track. Being in the first wave there would be no burning city to guide us, it being our job to start the fires.

Spot on zero hour red flares burst ahead. We were in the perfect position for the bombing run. The flak barrage opened up but the gunners hadn't quite got our height and the bursts were forming a carpet below us. Even so we could hear and feel the spent fragments of shrapnel rattling off the underside of the fuselage.

Stan selected a red TI dripping into cloud and released our blockbuster and incendiaries. Once the bombs were clear we headed south for the turning point at Reutlingen, then turned west for base. Six Lancasters were lost on this raid which caused serious damage to the central and eastern districts of Stuttgart including the important Bosch factory.

Chapter 10

ON A WING AND A PRAYER

The Ruhr Valley, somewhat perversely known as the 'Happy Valley', was in fact hated and feared by bomber crews. The ferocity of its defences, most especially the wall of flak and light surrounding Essen and the great Krupp works, made some bomber pilots have the urge to flinch and turn aside before reaching the aiming point. On 23 October we were briefed for a night raid on Essen and were to have very close contact with one of those 'Fringe Merchants' as they were called.

On the operations board in the briefing room, 20 Lancasters were listed in alphabetical order. Sgt Yule was chalked against S – Sugar 2. I was unique; all the other Captains were officers. Tonight's operation though would change that.

Bad weather had held up operations for the last three days and today there was no improvement. There was low cloud base and thick cloud up to over 20,000ft but Met had predicted that the high cloud would clear over Essen. That was enough for Butch Harris who was anxious to get on with the battle of the Ruhr.

This was another thousand-bomber raid and in fact the number of aircraft dispatched was the greatest number to any target so far. In normal visibility the sky over North Lincolnshire was a throbbing mass of bombers on a maximum effort like this. Climbing through thick cloud, you knew they were all there but could not see them. Occasionally a black shape loomed out of the mist, which necessitated quick avoiding action. The tension eased slightly when you stopped circling and steadied on to the first course.

Sugar 2 climbed steadily, 10,000ft, 15 then 18, our allotted bombing altitude. Still we were in thick cloud. I continued climbing to 22,000ft hoping to get in the clear but it was not to be. With a 13,000lb bomb load we had reached our ceiling and I gradually dropped back to 18,000ft.

Approaching Essen on a Northerly heading, we were still in cloud after nearly three hours when suddenly we burst into clear air. Far below us 10/10ths cloud nullified the searchlights but the flak barrage 10 miles ahead above the green dripping sky markers, seemed to fill every inch of sky.

Stan had asked for bomb doors open when suddenly Greg screamed, 'Down Jock!' The wireless operator was required to keep watch in the astrodome while in the target area. He had just popped his head up and was horrified to see another Lancaster directly above, disgorge its bomb load. I swung the control wheel to port and rammed it forward, at the same time kicking on full rudder. Don looked out to see a 4,000lb bomb smash through the starboard wing, slicing off 28ft of the trailing edge and carrying away the aileron. Fortunately the bomb had not sufficient time to fuse or we would have just been scraps of skin floating over Essen.

The impact of the bomb had straightened up Sugar's dive to port but I still had to keep on full left rudder and full remaining aileron just to stay level.

The Lancaster was vibrating badly as Stan dropped our bomb load on the green TIs. Closing the bomb doors we had to turn West to get on to a homeward heading. This was achieved with great difficulty. I found that if I stretched my left foot hard on the rudder pedal and yanked the control wheel as hard over as possible, Sugar 2 would just crab slowly to port. It seemed to take ages but we threaded through the flak bursts without sustaining any further damage and got on to the required course.

Leaving the barrage behind we were soon back in cloud. The situation was grim; vibration was so bad the instruments were barely readable. I had to steady the sprung instrument panel with my right hand to get an approximate idea of the aircraft's attitude. The gyrocompass was useless but I could just read the master compass repeater if steadied.

I was twisted in my seat keeping on hard left rudder and the control wheel turned fully to the left. If I had let either go the Lancaster would have done a continuous roll to starboard becoming uncontrollable.

With still nearly three hours to go, what I had dreaded happened. A bomber ahead of us in the cloud crossed in front and his slipstream twisted us starboard. With our wings nearly vertical we lost altitude fast. I could only strain for the extra half inch on the rudder and remaining aileron and wait. Slowly, so slowly, Sugar 2 righted herself but we had dropped 4,000ft.

Both starboard engines were now running rough as I pondered what to do when we got back to Wickenby. Should I bale the crew out over the airfield before heading the Lancaster out to sea and attempting to bale out myself? The circuit would be thick with returning bombers and we would have no chance if we hit a slipstream at low altitude.

Tubby piped up from the rear turret, 'Hey Jock, the shit's being shook out of me back here'. I told him in no uncertain terms to shut up, although I realised it was no fun being dragged backwards in a goldfish bowl and being rattled to bits.

I informed the crew that I was going to attempt a landing at base but that any of them could bale out if they wished. Each in turn said they would stay with me.

Nearing base, I called up Wickenby Control, informed them of the damage and stressed that a clear circuit was essential. We were at 10,000ft and still in thick cloud. Control informed me that cloud base was still only 800ft and would call me when all the other aircraft had landed and it was safe for us to descend.

Unknown to us then, Air Vice-Marshal Sir Edward Rice, Commander of No. 1 Group was following the drama in the Wickenby Control Tower.

Here, Gus our navigator was proving his worth. He was in complete command of our navigational aids and knew our position at all times. I still had the agonisingly slow struggle to turn on to each course as all turns had to be port. I gave Gus instructions where, in relation to the runway in use, I wanted to be when we broke cloud.

As we listened on the R/T to the 40 plus Lancasters from the two squadrons landing, we had another problem to think about. With the delayed landing time and the greatly increased drag on its airframe, Sugar 2 had burned up far more petrol than normal and our fuel was running very low. All the outer tanks were empty and Don estimated that what was left in the No. 1 tanks would give us only 15 minutes' flying time left.

At last clearance to land was given. On the descent I asked Don to lower 20 degrees of flap and the under-carriage. I had to know how Sugar 2 would react at landing speed with wheels down. I still had enough height to recover if she dropped the starboard wing in which case I would then have to land with our wheels retracted, on our belly. The test went all right, Don raised our wheels again and we continued our descent.

We broke cloud at exactly 800ft, in the position I wanted. What a relief it was to see outside again and not have to strain to read the vibrating green luminous instrument needles. There was one more heart stopping moment, when on the final approach and undercart down, the starboard wing did drop slightly due to normal turbulence. The Lancaster rapidly slipped off a few hundred feet before levelling up and the wheels screeched onto the tarmac.

Taxiing into dispersal, Don and I shut down the engines. Then, as the crew went out to look at the shattered wing, I undid my straps, stretched out, put my head back and relaxed. What bliss!

That night over Essen the Lancasters were each bombed up with one 4,000lb High Capacity (HC) bomb known as a 'Cookie' and nine 1,000lb Medium Capacity (MC) bombs. It was only really afterwards that we came to reflect that if the bomb aimer in the other Lanc. had released his load all in one go, then we were extremely lucky that we were hit by the 'Cookie' (as confirmed by Don) and not by one of the 1,000lb bombs. The reason for coming to this conclusion is that the way those bombs were fused, any one of them would almost certainly have exploded on impact with our wing. The 4,000lb bomb, however, was deemed to be so dangerous it was felt imperative that it had to be made doubly safe for the armourers and aircrew. This was done by installing three arming vanes which revolved and dropped off after the bomb reached its terminal velocity which it did after dropping over 10,000ft.

While on the subject it is worth mentioning that the 'Cookie' was reckoned to be probably the most effective bomb used by the RAF during the war. Used in conjunction with incendiaries they flattened many of Germany's urban centres and caused the terrible firestorms which devastated cities such as Hamburg and Dresden. The 1,000lb MC bombs on the other hand became the best performing general bombardment bombs to be used in the war and no fewer than 203,000 of these were dropped during 1944 alone.

Next day W/C Molesworth told me to put on my 'best blue', as Air Vice-Marshal Rice wanted to see me. I was driven over to No. 1 Group Headquarters at Bawtry, near Doncaster, about 30 miles from Wickenby.

Sir Edward Rice was not perhaps a Group leader as charismatic as Ralph Cochrane of 5 Group or Don Bennett with the Pathfinders, but he was a man who did the job Harris wanted doing – making sure that every serviceable aircraft bombed Germany at every possible opportunity. He visited airfields regularly, but was not known to chat with air or ground crews. He would tend to stick with the Station and Squadron Commanders.

AVM Rice was No. 1 Group Commander for two years and it was during this period that 1 Group rose to its pre-eminence in Bomber Command, probably due to his insistence for heavier bomb loads. There were times when the all up weight of the Lancasters (bombs and fuel) was exceeded by as much as 2,000lb. Despite a lack of official interest, he also collaborated with armament engineer Alfred Rose to produce the winning design of the Rose Rice twin 0.50in Browning tail turret for Lancasters in 1 Group.

Arriving at Bawtry Hall, a magnificent building standing in its own parklands, I wondered what exactly the Chief wanted to see me about. Molesworth had told me that Rice had seen for himself the extent of the damage on Sugar 2's wing. When ushered into his office I gave him the best salute I could muster. He beckoned me to sit down in a chair facing his desk. He was a man of about 50 years old, very military looking with a double row of World War One ribbons on his chest. He immediately put me at ease by smiling and asking various questions.

When he found out that we were still five miles from the aiming point when the bomb hit us, his smile vanished and he exploded with 'The bastard!' I found it difficult not to smile. After a few more searching questions about the control of the aircraft he shook my hand and said, 'Good show Yule, I'm putting you up for an immediate commission'.

Returning to Wickenby, I checked the Flight notice board and saw that we were listed on a battle order and that the briefing was early the next morning.

On 25 October after an early breakfast, we trooped into the briefing room. The target was Essen again. Take-off was delayed due to ground mist but visibility improved slightly and we took off in X-Ray 2 at 12.37pm. There was another long climb through thick cloud but at 16,000ft we burst through to beautiful sunshine and blue sky.

Cloud was not expected to clear over Essen so the attack was to be a 'Wanganui' which was the term for a blind attack in which the Pathfinders dropped flares to hang in the sky by parachutes. Each of these would be placed in a position so calculated that if the bombsights of the bombers above the cloud aimed at them, the resulting tonnage should hit the ground on target. X-Ray 2 was loaded with 11 1,000lb and four 500lb bombs.

Clouds still towered to over 15,000ft over Belgium and their tops were not smooth. Arriving in the area of the Ruhr, the flak barrage ahead was a mass of black puffballs against a pure white background of cloud. Stan decided to bomb one of the sky-markers, which was hanging by its chute above the cloud layer. On the bombing run Gus came out of his cabin, looked up at the sky above us, then looked at me, his eyes above the oxygen mask crinkled with laughter.

On our return above the North Sea, Don poured us both a cup of coffee from our flask. 'George' was in charge as we skimmed the cloud tops in the gathering dusk. A daylight raid was my 'cup of tea'. A photographic reconnaissance flight which took place after this raid showed severe damage to the remaining industrial concerns in Essen, particularly to the Krupps steelworks. The Borbeck pig iron plant ceased work completely and there was no record of any further production from this important section of Krupps. After these two raids on Essen much of its surviving industrial capacity was dispersed and the city lost its role as one of Germany's most important centres of war production

* * * * *

For the next few days bad weather restricted operations. Then Harris switched his attention to Cologne. We carried out two night raids on that much bombed city in quick succession on the 30 and 31 October. Both of these raids were flown through heavy cloud and the bombing was on sky-markers. We had Roger 2 back with its four new Mk 28 Merlin engines. It was a delight for Don and I to have the four engines synchronised and throbbing smoothly, especially on the way back.

On 2 November, in clearer weather, the Squadron was briefed to bomb Dusseldorf. The aiming point was to be in the northern half of the town where important steel firms were situated. Roger 2 had been bombed up with a 4,000lb cookie and 15 cans of incendiaries.

I climbed aboard and walked forward, throwing my observer type parachute behind the pilot's seat. I preferred this type to the pilot's because I could pack up the bucket seat with bundles of Window and get a better all round view. Whereas with the pilot's seat type chute hanging on my backside, packing up would have been more uncomfortable.

We took off at dusk and after two hours had crossed the Schelde estuary heading East. Wisps of stratus cloud cleared as we approached Dusseldorf. It was a clear night and I could see that there was a hot reception ahead – heavy flak, searchlights, the lot, a typical Ruhr target.

I had already seen an aircraft explode not too far ahead, presumably because of the flak, before we got to the target area. Then just as we were settling down for the run in to bomb, a Lancaster appeared on our port side as if from nowhere. It was flying at the same height and on the same heading, part silhouetted by a gaggle of searchlight beams beyond it. It was so near I could clearly see the pilot and engineer outlined in profile in their cockpit. I immediately eased over to starboard a bit which made Stan say, 'What are you doing Jock?' I said quickly, 'Another Lanc., too close on our port'. I kept an eye on the other Lancaster in case he changed course. He seemed unaware of us.

Then it happened. A flurry of flak came hurtling up between us (right through the space we would have been occupying!) and some of it obviously hit the other aircraft because I saw a thin streak of flame begin to stream back along its fuselage from somewhere near its starboard wing root. I watched fascinated as the flames thickened within split seconds, turning the Lancaster into a torch. Then the wing parted company and the rest fell away blazing and disappeared from my view.

It all happened so fast I could hardly believe it; then Stan's voice, 'Left left, – left left', took my attention back to the job in hand.

We dropped our load in the centre of four red target indicators, then I held the course for a few seconds to get a good photograph before pulling away from the target. Had that Lancaster not appeared when it did we might have been the one hit by the flak. In a sense he saved our lives although their crew all almost certainly perished.

On the return flight to base I had time to digest what I had seen. This was the closest I had been to the destruction of a four engined bomber and had been able to time the event from first strike to disintegration. It gave me quite a shock; I had thought a bomber crew would have had more time to get out from being set alight. I imagined if we had been hit and I had to scrabble behind my seat to find my parachute before making my way to the escape hatch in the nose. I vowed there and then to always wear a pilot type parachute which at least would give me a valuable few more seconds.

CHAPTER 11

THE KING'S COMMISSION

Returning from a week's leave, we were briefed for four consecutive operations which were all scrubbed due to appalling weather comprising winds of gale force, low cloud and rain. When finally, after the fifth briefing there was no last minute cancellation, the squadron took off on 18 November to attack the oil refineries at Wanne-Eickel on the Ruhr.

The weather cleared over the target and a successful attack was carried out. Many large explosions occurred, the flashes of which showed up the storage tanks clearly.

Approaching England on our return we flew into the bad weather again. Wickenby had closed up completely and we were diverted to Framlingham in Suffolk. This was the home of the American 390th Bomb Group, who flew B 17 Flying Fortresses.

Thirteen of the Squadron's Lancasters landed here and what a welcome we received. At the debriefing by US intelligence officers, mugs of coffee, cakes and cigarettes were liberally dispensed. Then a large crate was trundled in and broken open; it was filled with bourbon rye whisky. Glasses were filled with a large measure and we were informed that we could have as many tots as we wished so long as a signature was given for each one. Normally debriefing took 15 to 20 minutes but this one was lasting well over an hour. We could have spun it out even further but one drunken crew started a singsong at their table and the Americans, laughing, called a halt.

At breakfast next morning, and what a breakfast, there was as much bacon, eggs and beans as anyone wanted. At RAF stations, aircrew on operations got one fried egg as a special concession with their meal before and after each op, and when not on ops, dried egg or sweet porridge was the fare. When airborne we had flasks of coffee and packets of chocolate and also one orange each which became rock hard at 20,000ft.

The dried egg brings to mind an amusing story regarding our navigator Gus who went to the Netherlands on business some time in the 1960s. While there he met one of the grateful recipients of Operation Manna which took place from 29 April to 7 May 1945. A large part of Western Holland was still in German hands and the population was approaching starvation; in fact many old or sick people had already died. A truce was arranged with the local German commander and Bomber Command, including Lancasters from Wickenby, delivered 6,672 tons of food before the Germans surrendered and allowed ships and road transport to enter the area. This gentleman invited Gus to his home for dinner, and soon after arrival opened a cupboard and proudly brought out a packet of National Dried Egg. When a surprised Gus asked him why, if the Dutch were starving, it hadn't been eaten, he was told 'We weren't *that* hungry!' This story perhaps explains why getting the occasional real egg with our corned beef or spam was such a big deal for us at the time.

As we waited at Framlingham for the weather to clear we busied ourselves with various checks on Roger 2. Don was kept busy opening the bomb doors to let the yanks see the cavernous bomb bay. A Lancaster could carry nearly three times the tonnage of a Flying Fortress.

Late in the afternoon we got clearance for Wickenby and not long after all the Lancasters had landed, the weather clamped down again.

A week passed before the weather cleared. Then on 27 November we bombed the rail centre at Freiburg, south of Stuttgart, in bright moonlight. Two days later the squadron attacked Dortmund in daylight but bad weather caused poor marking by the Pathfinders.

On 3 December the squadron was sent to bomb the town of Heimbach in the Eiffel Region. I believe that this was intended to be in support of an American ground attack in this area and Roger 2 carried 14 1,000lb bombs. However, bad weather prevented the Master Bomber and Pathfinders from identifying the target and we were sent home with our full bomb loads. Landing with a full load of bombs certainly sharpens the concentration – the landings were excellent that day although the weather conditions were very poor.

* * * * *

I then learned that my commission had come through, backdated to 24 October, the day of my meeting with AVM Rice. I had to vacate the hut in which I had lived with the rest of the crew since we came to Wickenby, and go to the officers' site among the pine trees, on the far side of the domestic area. There was little difference in the accommodation and I missed the bickering and the humour of the crew around me. However, I appreciated the comfort of the officer's mess which was less crowded and better furnished than the sergeants', and there was some pleasure to be drawn from the rise in pay and status. My salary as a heavy bomber Captain, now holding King George VI's commission, was a few pennies over £20 a month.

I opened an overdraft with the Glyn Mills bank and went in to Lincoln to equip myself with uniform. I returned at lunchtime knowing that a briefing was laid on for 3pm. The target was Karlsruhe, close to the French border north east of Strasbourg, and we took off at 4.30pm in Roger 2.

After three hours flying we were on the bombing run when Frank reported a Messerschmitt 262 high on our port. Our intelligence bods had warned us that these very fast jet propelled fighters were now operating with the 'Wild

Boar units' of the German night fighters. As the bombs dropped it was the normal procedure for me to push the nose down, increase the speed and after giving a few seconds for the photograph, turn hard on to a new course. I had just got into the turn to a southerly heading when, looking back at the target, a Messerschmitt 109, clearly silhouetted against the fires in Karlsruhe, flashed under the starboard wing. He could not have been more than 20ft from us. Both gunners had been watching the ME 262 up on our port while the 109 pilot had been making his attack from our starboard. Fortunately my diving turn into him as he was lining up his guns had put him off completely, causing him to stuff his own nose down just missing us. I gave Tubby a bollocking for not picking him up. Frank had spotted the jet fighter and was watching him; Tubby should have been covering our other side.

Perhaps an explanation of what we did and did not know of the German night fighter tactics at that time will help inform the reader.

The Germans had reacted swiftly to our use of Window in the summer of 1943 by introducing two new defensive tactics, code named 'Wilde Sau' and 'Zahme Sau' – Wild Boar and Tame Boar. Wild Boars were single-engined fighters stationed close to the big cities which were sent into action using the various types of illumination available over the target areas. These were mainly the improved Messerschmitt 109s and Focke Wulf 190s. They carried no radar set and so once the pilot had taken off having been directed to the target city he was free of ground control. Accordingly any success he achieved was the result of his own roving efforts. Over some of the smaller targets the flak barrage would cease so that they did not shoot down their own fighters. Over the larger cities or conurbations, however, the box barrage carried on and the wild boars would operate just outside the flak, attacking the bombers approaching and leaving the target.

'Tame Boars' were twin-engine fighters, normally Junkers 88s and Messerschmitt 110s. These were fitted with the new airborne radar set Lichtenstein SN2 which could pick up and home on to a bomber from four miles. This range would, of course, be no use unless the fighters could be guided into the bomber stream by some other system. This system was as follows: the German night fighter controllers were aware, early in the evening of an operation, that a raid was pending. When we switched on our radio transmitters and H2S sets to warm up, while the aircraft were still on their dispersal sites, their monitoring service knew it. When the German Divisional Controllers gave the signal, the fighters were scrambled and instructed to orbit one of a number of radio beacons, selecting the beacon nearest to the predicted track of the raid. Then, as the raiders approached, the fighters would be in a position to enter the bomber stream and start picking up contacts on their radar. They were initially listening in to a running commentary from their controller who kept them informed of the track, speed and height of the bomber stream.

Our countermeasures team had by now fitted certain Lancasters within the special No. 100 Squadron with extra radio equipment and also included a fluent German speaker in the crew. He counterfeited the German controller's voice over a powerful transmitter, warning all German fighters to land because of the danger of fog, or other spurious instructions. When the Germans found out we were intervening in this way, they supplemented verbal orders with music so that, for example, a waltz meant that the bombers were in the Munich area, jazz meant Berlin, and so forth. When our German speaker was frustrated in this way, he could bring in another countermeasure jamming the German ground to night fighter running commentary by transmitting the noise of the Lancaster's engines with microphones installed there.

The conventional method of attack in use by the 'tame boars' was the *von unter hinten*, literally from under and behind. This was a long approach on radar, ending in a visual sighting. This was quite easy for the German pilot once he got close because of the Lancaster's glowing orange exhaust stubs. The fighter then approached from below and astern in a slightly nose up attitude, aiming its fixed forward cannons at the bomber's fuselage. Since the bombers usually carried a thin-skinned 'cookie' in addition to several smaller bombs, a strike here would often cause a massive explosion frequently destroying the fighter as well. Accordingly the tame boars developed a new form of attack – the *schrage musik* attack. This I did not know of until after the war, but in retrospect I realised that I must have witnessed many bombers destroyed by this method. In one raid to Nuremberg on the night of 16 March 1945, which I will describe later, I personally saw 10 Lancasters shot down in this way. In fact I now think that the Lancaster which I described being destroyed at the end of the previous chapter was the victim of such an attack because with hindsight I don't recall seeing the type of explosion which you would have expected from flak. If so then had that fighter been lining up on me and then switched his attention to the doomed Lanc when I moved over to starboard?

Schrage musik – which translated as jazz music or more literally slanting music, involved a pair of upward firing cannons mounted behind the fighter's cockpit. The German pilot, with a gun sight in the roof of his cockpit, aimed from below, usually with plenty of time for accuracy, at a point between the two port engines of the bomber. When he fired, the exploding cannon shells would set the bomber's fuel tanks on fire and the fighter pilot, knowing that an explosion would soon follow, could pull away immediately without himself being blown up. If the bomber crew baled out quickly enough they might escape alive from a 'schrage music' attack, but that probability was remote.

Martin Middlebrook, in his excellent book on the Nuremberg raid of 30/31 March 1944, states the following:

'So successful was *schrage musik* that few British aircraft managed to return and tell of being attacked by it. Those who did so probably did not know how they had been hit because the upward-firing guns used only very faint tracer. And so the Germans were able to use this weapon for many months without Bomber Command being aware of it. This surprised the Germans, for many civilians worked on the night-fighter airfields in the occupied countries and it was assumed that details of the installation would be passed by the Resistance to England.'

As I said above, I did not know of the *schrage musik* method of attack until after the war. Bear in mind, however, that this tactic was being used by the Germans by March 1944 at the latest and that I still didn't know about it when my tour ended a full year later! I have my suspicions therefore that our top brass may have become aware of what was happening but took a decision not to advise the bomber crews for what they perceived to be a very good reason. Had the pilots been aware of this threat they would assuredly have been weaving about all over the sky above enemy territory long before they got near the target rather than focusing on keeping their position within the stream. Thus the danger of mid-air collisions on night raids (already a major risk and the cause of a significant number of lost bombers) would have manifestly increased. I for one would definitely not have serenely relied on 'George' the auto-pilot to nearly the same extent had I known of the *schrage musik* threat. Accordingly in retrospect I think that our high command may have deemed that the *schrage musik* threat was in a sense the lesser of two evils. That is just my suspicion, however, and I have no proof of this. Perhaps one day the truth will come out.

All 16 aircraft from our squadron returned safely from the Karlsruhe raid around midnight. The marking and bombing were reported as accurate and among individual buildings destroyed was the important Durlacher machine-tool factory.

* * * * *

On the afternoon of 22 December 1944 the Squadron was briefed for a raid on Koblenz, a city situated at the confluence of the Rhine and Mosel rivers. The aiming point was to be the Mosel railway yards.

For the last few days, persistent fog had curtailed operations and as the weather was similar we fully expected another scrub. Take off was delayed for half an hour but then to our surprise at 15:38 hours we got take off clearance.

I could just see either side of the runway and a little way ahead to line up the Lancaster and set the gyrocompass. In conditions such as those on take-off – rushing into fog, it was imperative not to allow the aircraft to develop a swing. With 13 1,000lb bombs under your feet and tanks full of 100-octane petrol, a bad swing could collapse the under-carriage and it could be 'curtains', so you watched the gyrocompass like a hawk and corrected the slightest deviation by manipulation of the throttle levers.

As we climbed away through cloud and knowing the weather was deteriorating, I wondered where we could be diverted to on our return as it seemed the whole of Britain was affected by fog.

We flew in silence except for the steady roar of the engines. Three hours had passed and the only talk was when Gus gave me course alterations and estimated times of arrival. Then, on our run in to Koblenz, Stan asked for bomb doors open. Visibility was good and there was very little cloud below us but we could not see any Pathfinder markers although it was after zero hour. We could now see bombs exploding and black blobs of flak began to appear when suddenly six red flares with green stars burst directly ahead. We were in the perfect position and Stan bombed the centre of the markers without having to give me any corrections to course. The flak wasn't too bad so we did not do our usual 'bat out of hell' departure from the target.

Thick fog had indeed increased over most of England and on our return leg Greg received a message diverting us to Bradwell Bay, on the Essex coast.

This was the first experience I had of landing in thick fog at an airfield using FIDO, which stands for 'Fog Investigation and Dispersal Operation'. This consisted of long lengths of pipe and burners, parallel with the runway and about 50 yards from it. The burners were about 150 yards apart and extended along each side of the runway. When operating, the system burns several tons of petrol per minute.

Letting down through thick fog, it was with some trepidation that I lowered the undercart before seeing the glow through the fog and at about 100ft we broke into clear air. The system shot two walls of flame up to 50ft as I brought Lancaster X-Ray 2 in between them. It was very impressive and awe inspiring.

The next morning, fog was still blanketing most of England and it was not until the afternoon that it was considered clear enough for Wickenby to accept us back. Circling the airfield prior to landing I thought I saw a quarry hole near the bomb dump which had not been there before, but it was still quite misty and I did not mention it to the crew. After landing we learned of the tragedy.

Two hours after we had taken off for Koblenz the previous afternoon, Flying Officer R. Preece had returned in Lancaster E-Easy 2 with his port inner engine feathered and useless. Wickenby was now covered in thick fog and he was diverted to Leeming in Yorkshire, which had better visibility but it too was deteriorating fast. No one knows exactly why, but it was assumed that in his anxiety to get to Leeming he turned too fast and got disorientated in the fog, stalled and crashed near the bomb dump. This was the crater I had seen before landing but there was nothing left of the Lancaster. The largest parts ever found were the rear gunner's seat and an airman's foot in a flying boot. (Although it is possible to turn steeply into one or two dead engines in a Lancaster, it is a different matter with a full bomb load.)

F/O Preece was a flamboyant character who had a superb painting of a Chinese dragon on the back of his Irvine jacket. I don't know if he had painted it himself but it was a beautiful job, all red, gold, silver and green.

That night in the mess, Jock Craigie, the Squadron Signals leader, told me the following:

'After the main briefing the signallers returned to their section office for a more detailed signals briefing. Having completed this, I distributed their 'Gen.' satchels containing Bomber code, etc., each satchel being numbered and each signaller having to sign for the one given to him. This completed, I wished them all good luck and they all left the office with the exception of one signaller by the name of Stapleton in Preece's crew. I said "What's the matter Taffy?" (he was a Welshman) and he said "Sir, could I please change my 'Gen.' satchel?" I said, "Why, what is wrong with the one you have signed for?" He replied that he was superstitious and had been given No. 13. I said, "Of course Taffy take No. 22", which he did, signed for it and went off to join his crew.'

Had Stapleton a premonition of impending disaster? Jock Craigie certainly thought so, as he said he had never seen him so worried looking, and thought it was not just the No. 13 satchel.

Persistent fog curtailed operations for the next few days until our leave was due. I was glad not to have to deliver bombs over the Christmas period.

While on operations, aircrew were given seven days leave every six weeks and I invariably went home to Aberdeen which entailed getting a bus to Lincoln and from there a train north via York. On this leave Stan and Greg

My parents' wedding photograph, 1907. This is the only extant photograph I have of my father.

My mother, sisters and brother at 57 Jasmine Terrace, 1917. Left to right: Sandy, Muriel and Maggie.

In my pageboy uniform on the roof of the Forsyth Hotel, Aberdeen, 1937.

Aircrew intake at Regent Park, London, 28 February 1942. I am second row, fourth from right, sitting next to Corporal Croswell.

Gordon Cummins (The Blackout Ripper).

A Catalina Flying Boat.

My first solo in a Catalina Flying Boat, Pensacola, Florida, April 1943. (Taken by Paul Thompson.)

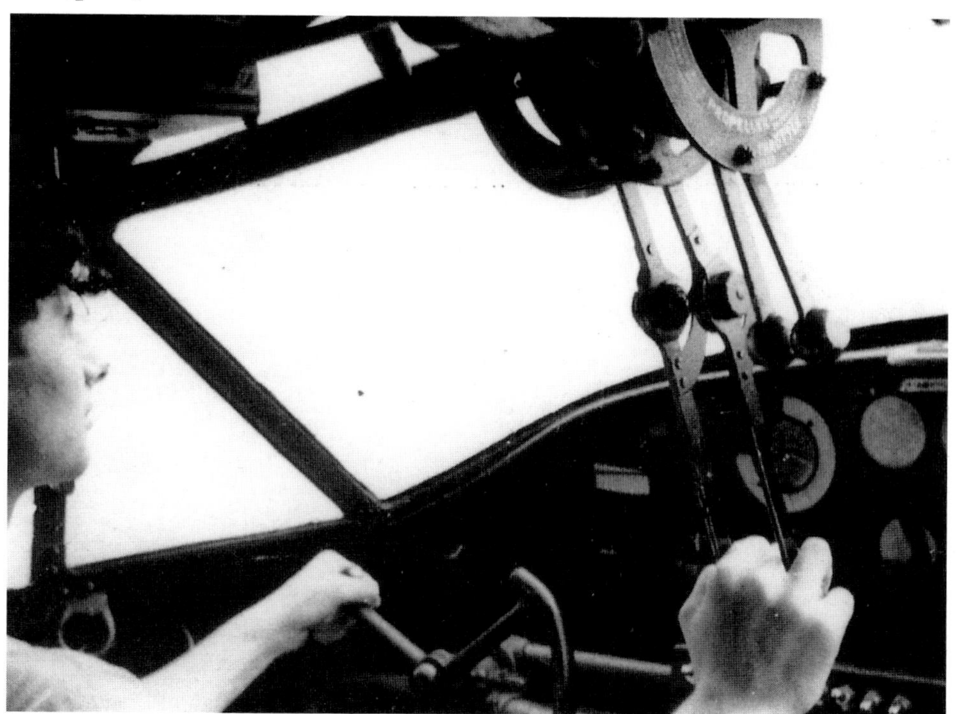

In my RAF student's uniform with newly gained wings, Pensacola, June 1943.

Rudi Balzer with Arthur Lee at the Lancaster crash site near Katzenelnbogen, Germany in October 1984.

Rudi Balzer in 1943.

Air Vice-Marshall Sir Edward Rice (Commander AOC 1 Group 1942–45).

Frank Fathers, Greg Mayes, Stan Moore, Tubby Clayton, Don Leader, posing with a 4,000lb 'Cookie' bomb.

Stan, Tubby, Frank, Greg, Self, Don. This was taken after our first operation to Saarbrucken on 6 October 1944. It had been Roger 2's 53rd operation. She went on to complete 101 operations and became the only Lancaster on 626 Squadron to do a 'ton-up'.

Frank Fathers, mid-upper gunner (within turret dome).

Arthur Clayton, tail-gunner (within rear turret).

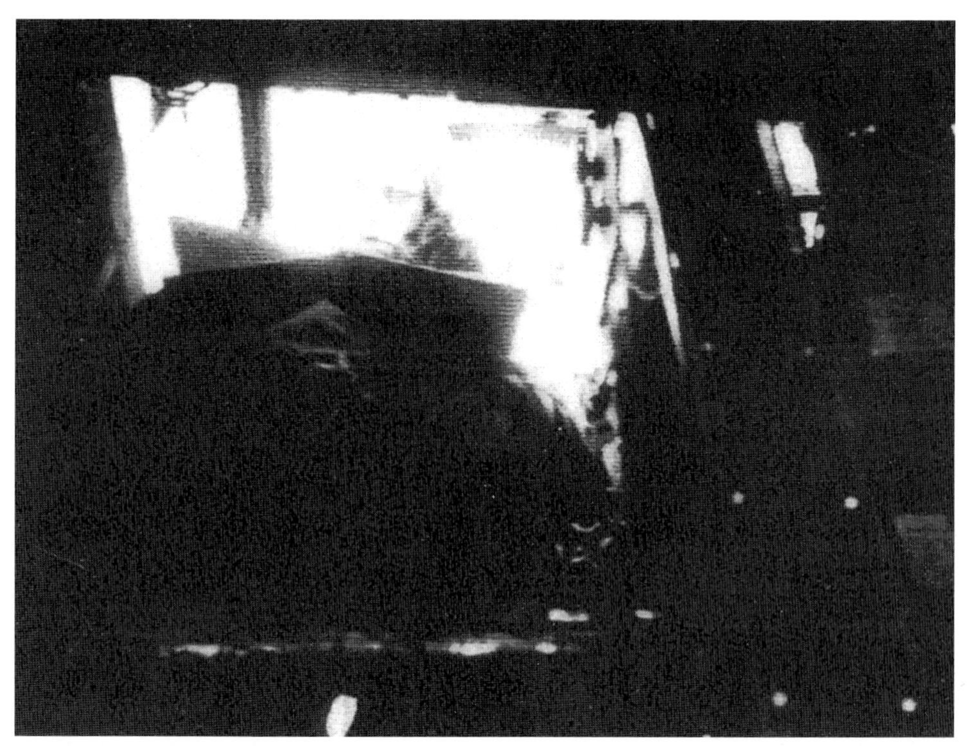

Don Leader, flight engineer.

Stan Moore, bomb aimer.

This is me in the cockpit of Roger 2 with the 'Bennet's Beavers' logo clearly visible.

Snow clearance at Wickenby – January and February 1945.

On such occasions all aircrew plus groud crews who could be spared, would turn out to man brooms and shovels, working round the clock in order to clear runways and dispersals – an arduous back breaking task. For the Aussies, many of whom had never even seen snow, it was an ideal opportunity to let off steam and indulge in high spirited snow fights, which ended up Australia versus Great Britain.

It was cold enough for those huddled round the single stove in the Nissen huts but for those working on the Lancasters, that winter was an unforgettable experience.

612 Squadron pilots before the Battle of Britain display, 1949. Back row, left to right: Nigel McLean, Bill Innes, Len Cherry, Jock Dalgleish, Doug Robertson, Pat Pattullo. Front row: Roddy Robertson, Johnny Milne, Alan Mitchell, Roddy McKay, Self.

612 Squadron pilots in dress uniform, 1950. From left: Roddy Robertson, Jim Healy, Self, Trevor Smith, Doug Robertson, Roddy McKay, Bill Innes, Doug Rutherford. Kneeling: Alan Mitchell, Bill Thom.

With Professor Reginald Victor Jones.

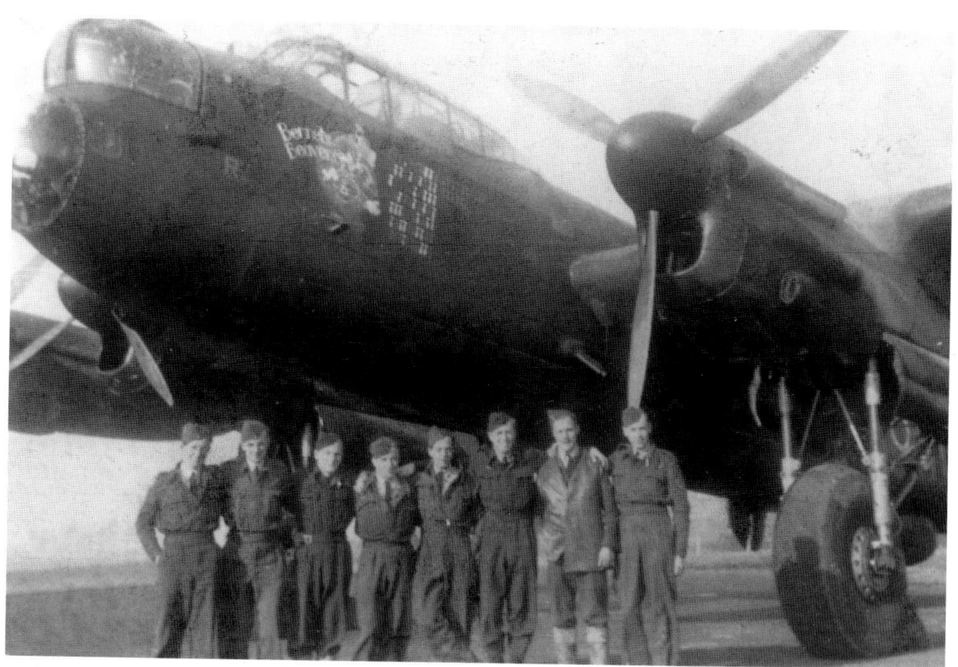

Left to right: Self, Gus Marbaix, Greg Mayes, Tubby Clayton, Frank Fathers, Stan Moore, F/Sgt McPherson (i/c ground crew), Don Leader. This photograph was taken in front of Roger 2 following the raid to Dresden on 13 February 1945.

Before and 37 years after.

Left to right: Stan Moore, Arthur Clayton, Greg Mayes, Self, Tony Marbaix, Gordon Leader. Beside the Wickenby Memorial, September 1982.

Flying Janitor Is The Schoolboys' Hero

HERO of Ruthrieston J.S. Schoool pupils is janitor Royan Yule. At week-ends he dons the light blue uniform of a flight lieutenant of the 612 R .Aux. A.F. and flies Vampire jets from R.AF. Dyce.

In 1941 Royan gave up his apprenticeship as a marine engineer to join the Royal Air Force. He was then nineteen.

He trained in the U.S. and Canada and gained a commission as flying officer in 1944. The following year, while with Bomber Command, he was awarded the D.F.C. He completed thirty - seven sorties over enemy territory.

Flying Janitor is the Schoolboys' 'Hero'. (*Aberdeen Evening Express* – 1955)

came with me and after spending Christmas Day at Wickenby we got up to my home town in time to celebrate Hogmanay.

Stan and Greg got free accommodation at the Caledonian Hotel on Union Terrace. Lord Nuffield provided this perk for Bomber Command operational aircrews in various hotels around Britain. Few Australian aircrews reached Aberdeen during the war and with their distinctive dark blue uniforms they attracted quite a lot of attention. With that and enjoying an all night Scottish Hogmanay first footing session, they both avowed it the best leave ever.

My girlfriend Winnie had also managed to get tickets for us all to see the show *Panama Hattie* in HMTheatre, starring Ben Lyon and Bebe Daniels. Max Wall (at that time relatively unknown) was the brilliant dancer comedian. Although the blackout was still in force, the general mood in the city was now markedly different to that which had prevailed just under three years previously when I had boarded the train to London at the start of my great adventure. There had been bad times since then and indeed Aberdeen's biggest air raid of all had taken place on the night of 21 April 1943 when I was in America and which resulted in a death-toll of 125 with another 235 injured. In place of those dark days, however, there was now a firm belief that ultimate victory was virtually assured. The cinemas, dance halls and pubs were all going strong and I introduced Stan and Greg to a few traditional Aberdeen pubs. These included the Pittodrie Bar and the Scotia near my home, and the Grill and 'Graveyard' bars on or adjacent to Union Street. The standard tipples were McEwans or Youngers beer and either Watsons rum or more often the cheap 'Red Hackle' whisky which was a brand of firewater which I don't think you can get nowadays. If you were in the money then you would tend to choose Bells or one of the other more expensive brands.

All too soon though, it was time to get back to Lincolnshire and find out what next lay in store.

CHAPTER 12
ROYAN

Returning from leave on 4 January we were immediately put on the battle order for that night, briefing just before midnight. I was amazed to see my Christian name chalked in large letters above the route board as the target. I had been unaware until then of any place called Royan.

This was a tragic raid with a strange and disputed background. Royan was a town situated at the mouth of the River Gironde in which a stubborn German garrison was still holding out, preventing the Allies from using the port of Bordeaux. General De Gaulle had given the task of besieging the town with 12,000 men of the French Resistance commanded by Free French officers appointed by him. The Commander of the German garrison recognised the Resistance units as regular forces and the normal rules of warfare were observed. The French, lacking artillery, made little progress with their siege. The German Commander gave the inhabitants of the town the opportunity to leave but many preferred to stay and look after their homes. It is believed that there were 2,000 civilians still in the town at the time of the raid.

The request that Bomber Command should attack the town had a tortuous background and the version given here (which I have taken from the 'Bomber

Command War Diaries'), may be open to dispute. On 10 December 1944, a meeting took place at the town of Cognac between French officers and an American officer from one of the tactical air force units in France. After a meal, at which much alcohol is supposed to have been consumed, the American officer suggested that bombing should soften up the German garrison at Royan. The French assured him that the only civilians remaining in the town were collaborators – which was not correct.

The suggestion that the town be bombed was passed to SHAEF (Supreme Headquarters Allied Expeditionary Force), which decided that the task be given to Bomber Command: 'To destroy a town strongly defended by enemy and occupied by German troops only.' It is said that SHAEF ordered a last minute cancellation because of doubts about the presence of civilians but the order, if issued, was not received by Bomber Command in time.

The attack was carried out by two waves of over 300 Lancasters from 1 Group, in good visibility, at 5.30am on 5 January. Local reports show that between 85 and 90 per cent of the small town was destroyed. The number of French civilians killed was given as '500 to 700'. The number of Germans killed was 50. A local truce was arranged and, for the next 10 days, there was no fighting while the search for survivors in wrecked houses continued.

There were many recriminations. Bomber Command was immediately exonerated. The American air-force officer who passed on the original suggestion to SHAEF was removed from his Command. The bitterest disputes took place among the Free French officers and accusations and counter accusations continued for many years after the war. A French general committed suicide. De Gaulle in his Memoirs, blamed the Americans: 'American bombers, on their own initiative, came during the night and dropped a mass of bombs.' The German garrison did not surrender until 18 April.

Learning of the foregoing after the war, it gave me some consolation that our crew was not responsible for the death of even one French civilian.

After the briefing, we collected our gear and were driven to Q – Queenie 2's dispersal. While we had been on leave, Roger 2 had received flak damage and was undergoing repairs. Light snow was falling as we climbed aboard and carried out the pre-flight checks. The bomb load was one 4,000lb 'cookie' and 16 500lb bombs.

Taking off at 2.15am, Gus gave me a course of 190 degrees to steer and I climbed up to our bombing altitude of 10,000ft. Crossing the English coast east of Portsmouth, we entered dense cloud and encountered severe icing, the like of which I had never experienced before or since. First, the needle of the air-speed indicator dropped to zero. Ice had formed in the pitot head tube and although there is a small electrical heater there, it could not cope with those conditions. Then ice formed on the propeller roots and as it slipped down the blades, it was thrown off at high speed, hitting the fuselage just behind me like machine gun bullets. During this time, the leading edges of the wings and tail plane had coated with half an inch of clear steel-like ice. I tried climbing out of the icing layer but with full power on, Queenie 2 could only maintain height. She was wallowing and reacting sluggishly to the controls. I could not risk taking on any more ice so started to descend. At 7,000ft the cloud started to thin out and eventually cleared and we had passed through the cold front.

The Pathfinder Mosquitoes had positioned red target indicators directly over Royan. Stan asked for bomb doors open and as we were running up on the target, still at 7,000ft, covered in ice, Queenie 2 still could not gain height. With the red TIs in his bombsight, Stan pressed the bomb release tit and nothing happened – the bomb electrical release catches were all frozen. I told Stan that I would go round again and asked Greg to operate the manual release on the 4,000lb blockbuster when Stan gave the signal.

On our first run up to the target, a German gun boat in the estuary had been firing at us and I asked Stan to aim at him on this run. I did not want to chance being hit by any more 'friendly bombs' as had happened over Essen. We must have come close to being hit from the Lancasters above on this compact target. Stan gave directions and as we lined up on the gunboat it started firing again. A string of flaming oranges came at us, slowly at first then screaming past us as they got nearer.

Then Stan said, ‘ OK Greg let it go…now!’ With relief I felt the lurch as the Cookie fell away. The flaming oranges stopped coming and Stan, laughing said ‘I missed him but he’s got a bloody good soaking’. I said we would do another run on him and asked Greg to try and get a couple of 500 pounders away. Tubby said, ‘Jock, can I have a go at him with my guns?’ I gave him my consent but I knew 303 bullets would have little effect at this range. We carried out the run and after the two bombs dropped away Tubby blazed away with his four guns. Stan reported another two near misses. I said, ‘Give me a course Gus, we are going home’. By this time the ice had started to clear from the wings. It was daylight when we landed with still over half the bomb load in the bomb bay.

It was after 10am before I got to bed, and was fast asleep as soon as my head touched the pillow. It seemed only minutes later when the bat-woman shook my shoulder and informed me that I had to report for briefing at 2pm. I looked at my watch and saw that it was 1.30pm.

Fifteen of the squadron’s crews were briefed to bomb the rail marshalling yards at Neuss, just west of Dusseldorf. In the event only 10 of us got off as the armourers could not cope with completing the job in such a short period. Roger 2 had been patched up from the flak damage sustained on the 29 December, and we took off at 3.30pm.

Nine-tenths cloud covered the target and Stan bombed red and green parachute flares five minutes after zero hour. We were at 20,000ft and the flak was bursting mostly below us as I closed the bomb doors and turned on to a westerly course. We had just crossed the battle lines north of Antwerp when there was a thump and a 500lb bomb (which had been ‘hung up’ on its mounting) dropped on to the bomb doors. As I mentioned earlier, 4,000lb blockbusters have three arming vanes which revolve and drop off as they fall but 500 and 1,000lb bombs have a short cable and as they fall from their mounts, the safety pin is pulled out. Therefore the bomb rolling about on our bomb doors was live and if its detonator jarred we were all history. I asked Gus how long before we were over the sea and he said five minutes. The ominous rumble continued. I opened the bomb doors and the bomb fell away. I reckoned that the chances of the bomb killing us was far, far greater than killing some farm worker on the Dutch – Belgium border.

Back again for interrogation; this was the best time of all, when something like euphoria seemed to possess everyone. The good feeling dissipated, however, when at the end of the debriefing a battle order was produced which included us. We also learned that the refuelling crews had orders to pump the maximum load of petrol into the Lancaster's tanks – 2,154 gallons, almost the whole of the petrol bowser's load, for one aircraft.

* * * * *

At the briefing on 7 January, the red ribbon on the map showed the reason for full tanks. The target was Munich, deep in the heart of Bavaria. Roger 2's load was a blockbuster and nine cans of incendiaries.

Snow showers delayed take-off, but the weather cleared and at 6.23pm we were airborne. With a strong tail wind we soon made up lost time, and by the turning point at Soissons, north east of Paris, had caught up with the main bomber stream and I was able to throttle back, conserving fuel for the long return against head winds.

Coming up to our last turning point before the target, just slightly north of the Swiss border, Gus gave me a course of 085 degrees for Munich; we still had 125 miles to go.

Approaching the target at 17,000ft there was a layer of smooth cloud at 10,000ft below us, lit up by many searchlights shining on its underside. I glanced up and spotted four Focke Wulf 190s at 10 o'clock high. We were in the perfect position for them to attack us and to them we must have looked like a big black moth crawling over a white sheet.

Considering there were over 600 Lancasters on this raid, there were surprisingly few near us that the fighters might choose instead of us. After informing the crew of the FW190s I instructed Tubby and Don to keep searching our starboard quarters while Frank trained his guns on the enemy fighters and was ready for them coming in.

Our bomb doors were open and Stan was giving directions for the run up to the TIs. I was thinking that the flak wasn't too bad and that the fighters might come in when a few shells burst close on our port. The port outer engine immediately wreathed in flames with the propeller windmilling. Stan was still giving directions so I thumped Don on the shoulder and pointed to the port outer. He immediately pressed the graviner switch which put the fire out on the engine and feathered the propeller.

The extensive glow of many fires was shining through the cloud as Stan released our bomb load sighted on the centre of six red and green flares. The FW190s had wheeled out of sight as I closed the bomb doors and turned south for the turning point at Innsbruck. The 'wild boars' would now know our route out so we would have to be extra vigilant.

North of Innsbruck, Gus gave me a course of 280 degrees, which would take us very near the Swiss border. We were now flying into very strong headwinds and with only three engines we were in great danger of lagging behind the main bomber stream and becoming a straggler. If we had been attacked I would have had no compunction about violating Swiss neutrality and diving into their airspace. Although we flew past numerous lines of fighter flares we did not fortunately see any more enemy fighters.

The long drag back to base took five hours and 20 minutes from the target, a total of nine hours and 15 minutes in the air. All the other Lancasters had landed by the time we were in the circuit, which was just as well, as we had very little fuel left and I was thankful to be able to go straight in.

Two of our Lancasters were missing from the 18 lost that night, F/O Stroh and F/O Smith. Later we were informed that F/O Smith, a Canadian, flying Lancaster Sugar 2, had collided with another Lancaster at the turning point at Soissons. (Sugar 2 was the Lancaster in which we got hit by the bomb over Essen.)

Most of F/O Smith's crew (with the exception of himself and the rear gunner, W. McLean) managed to bale out successfully and were taken to local French farms before being conducted to American army units for first aid. They were later flown home, reporting back to 626 Squadron on 15 January.

F/O Smith was killed in the crash and the fate of McLean, the rear gunner, is unknown, as neither he nor the turret had been found by the time the surviving crew returned home. They did not witness the crash of their aircraft. Local inhabitants informed them that the aircraft broke cloud and approached the town of Laon at a low altitude and in a shallow dive. A burst of power just enabled it to clear the town and crash into a railway cutting at 20:30 hours, where it burst into flames and finally blew up at 21:00 hours. The body of the captain was found 50ft from the wreck still wearing an unopened seat type chute; he must have tried to jump at the last moment.

One of the surviving crew members, Geoff Magee, the Aussie Wireless Operator, had a book of poems published in 1991 titled *Bombs gone and Other Poems.* Stan Moore was instrumental in getting me in touch with him but sadly I never did manage to take up his kind offer to spend a holiday with him in Australia and he has since passed on. I would like, however, to include one of his poems here which neatly sums up my own feelings regarding the extent to which our crew all very much depended on one another to get the job done and also to give us the best chance of survival:

The Seven Crew Members

The pilots just steered those big bombers you know,
It was the rest of the crew that made the things go,
The pilot just sat there and twiddled the wings,
While the engineer fiddled with switches and things.

Of course the Bomb Aimer knew they were there just for him,
To deliver his bombs and to keep the right trim,
And the Nav was quite sure his job was the best,
Giving courses to steer from his snug little nest.

While the W/Op was quite certain it was only he,
could get fixes and courses while over the sea,

And both Gunners were certain their jobs were the best,
They looked all around them and guarded the rest.

But the point of this story, I want you to see,
Was it took a team effort to win victory.

* * * * *

I awoke at noon to find that snow had been falling steadily and a vast whiteness covered the countryside. I walked to the Flight Office and checked that there was no battle order before carrying on to Roger 2's dispersal to check on the damage from the flak over Munich.

Meeting the Flt/Sgt in charge of the ground crew, he said, 'Bloody hell Sir, you took a battering last night didn't you? Look at all these holes'. He took me round Roger 2's port side pointing out the damage, saying, 'Of course the port outer engine is completely buggered and will have to be replaced, and as for patching up you won't be flying this kite for a week or two'. He sounded so aggrieved I had to say, 'Don't blame me, blame the bloody Germans'. He then laughed and said that actually the lads and him were surprised there was no blood to clean up as well.

Perhaps an interesting postscript to the Munich raid is that in 2001 I visited that city on a short break with my son. I have to say that I thoroughly enjoyed the whole trip from the marvellous museums to the great beer and Oompah band music in Bierkellers such as the Hofbrauhaus. In the latter establishment they incuded in their menu literature an account of the limited damage to the building caused by bomber raids in World War Two. However, I thought it best to keep quiet about my own role in that!

For the next few days there were numerous snow showers and all aircrews were organised under their captains to clear the snow off the aircraft and dispersal sites. By now Roger 2 was in the hangar so we had to do the needful for our secondary aircraft X-Ray 2. After the dispersal sites had been cleared, aircrews and ground crews who could be spared were sent to shovel snow off the runways. It was very hard work but there were surprisingly few grumbles.

* * * * *

On 13 January, ops were ordered for three aircraft from our squadron to carry out mine laying and 15 for bombing. Both operations, however, were cancelled after lunch because of the weather.

Next day ops were on again and F/O Lucas, F/O Rodger and myself were detailed for the mine laying sortie. The other 15 crews were briefed to bomb the Leuna synthetic oil plant at Merseberg, near Leipzig.

Germany had to supply its forces in Norway with regular supplies and to get to Oslo from the main port of Kiel, their ships had to pass through one of three well-marked channels. In the middle there was the Great Belt, over in the East there was a channel between Copenhagen and Malmo and in the West there was a bottleneck channel at Middelfart.

On 14 January, just before 8pm, off we went. We had to plant our mines in the middle channel between the islands of Zealand and Funen. Our Lancaster X-Ray 2 was loaded with six 2,000lb mines, which were virtually sweep proof. They were known as vegetables and could be dropped in fairly deep water and even if the ship was some distance away, the force of the explosion was such that it would practically always lift it out of the water.

The trip itself was uneventful. Although cloud covered the mining area, Gus got good fixes of the islands from the H2S radar and Stan operated the timing release. The Great Belt should have been well and truly straddled.

On our return halfway over the North Sea, Greg received a message diverting us to Charter Hall. Bomber command had mounted several different operations that night and really bad weather was affecting the bomber bases. Fourteen aircraft crashed in England and a further 17 bombers were lost through enemy action making a total of 31 aircraft lost for the night.

The three minelayers from 626 Squadron all landed at Charter Hall. This was a small training station between Greenlaw and Duns on the Scottish-

English border. Having to cater for 21 men at short notice at two o 'clock in the morning stretched the Station's resources to their limit but we were adequately fed under the circumstances. Not so the sleeping arrangements; we got one blanket each (that's all they had to spare) and we had to doss down in a derelict gym hut which had no doors. Although we had our flying clothing, it was bitterly cold lying on a bare floor with an Arctic like wind blowing through the building. Stan and Greg, the only two Australians in the three crews, huddled together like husky dogs and shared their blankets.

In the morning after a wash with cold water, we had breakfast, which consisted of toast and margarine and mugs of hot tea. Feeling much better, the good-humoured banter returned among the three crews. Sadly, all 14 of the other two crews would be dead in just over four weeks from now.

Word was then received that Wickenby could accept our return and so we took off and landed there at lunchtime. The ground crews immediately set to, refuelling and bombing up. However, there followed a frustrating spell of bad weather with alternately snow showers and long spells of fog. That would not have been so bad but operations were repeatedly ordered and cancelled so that we could not get off the station for a booze up.

CHAPTER 13
THE BEGINNING OF FEAR

After four and a half months on operations we had completed 20 missions and had only 10 more to complete our first tour, or so we thought then! By now we were one of the most experienced crews on the squadron and had been allotted a 'second dickey' to give him operational experience.

On 28 January we were briefed for a night raid on Stuttgart with P/O Warner, a New Zealander, as second pilot. The aiming point was to be the Zuffenhausen district where the Hirth aero-engine factory and the important Bosch works were situated.

Remembering the cool reception I received from F/O Winder's crew on my 'second dickey' trip, I made a point of introducing Bob Warner to each member of the crew when each in turn shook his hand. None of the crew was overly superstitious, as far as I knew; no lucky charms, favourite mascots or anything. It was supposed to be a superstitious ritual to relieve oneself over the tail wheel for luck. We all did it but to me it was just somewhere to aim on a bleak windswept dispersal site. So carrying the dreaded 'second dickey' should not make this operation any different as far as we were concerned.

We took off at 8pm, and were running up to the target at 20 minutes to midnight at a height of 20,000ft. Far below cloud covered the area but the sky was well lit with sky marker flares, red/yellow and red/purple. Well to the south the Germans were also firing dummy target indicator rockets into the air but they were much inferior to our own pyrotechnics and were the wrong colour combinations.

As Stan gave directions prior to 'bombs away' we were passing through a very tight flak barrage. I glanced across at Warner and saw him bouncing about trying to see everything that was going on, apparently unafraid. Then I realised that I was, unconsciously, screwing myself up in a ball to make myself as small a target as possible for the unseen red-hot flying shrapnel – a futile reaction if ever there was one.

On the long drag back to base, I had cause to reflect on four months of operations which were definitely now having an effect on me. On my initial raid I had been just like Warner and I wondered if back on that night in September, F/O Winder had been scrunching himself up going through the flak over Frankfurt. He probably had but nevertheless I found it disconcerting that I was not the hardened, fearless bomber pilot I had imagined myself to be. Before landing, just after 3am, I was consoling myself with the thought that I was maybe scared but never terrified.

Next day I made the usual entries in my logbook and operations sheet. The latter read:

Date 28. 1. 45 Time 08:10
A/C PA 990 UM – R2 Progressive total op hours 131.40
Captain Self
Target Stuttgart
Sortie No. 21 Remarks D.C.O.

As 30 sorties constituted the operational tour, Stuttgart marked the ⅔rd point for us (the Captain's second dickey op does not count, so he does 31).

Not that this achievement held any more than mathematical significance. At this stage I was approaching my lowest ebb and had ceased counting the number of operations left. So far as I could see, we would go on flying until we were killed and there wasn't any point in teasing oneself with the prospect of ultimate safety.

It wasn't that I was losing faith in the crew or myself. We were recognised as one of the best crews on the squadron; our bombing photographs proved that. I knew that I could fly and land the Lancaster in really horrible weather but I also realised by then that no matter how skilful the pilot and crew were, luck was the overriding factor in whether a crew survived to complete a tour or not.

The main risk, or so I thought at that time, was the all-obliterating flak burst when going through the barrage of a heavily defended German city. Every crew became hardened to seeing other bombers blowing up or going down in flames and felt a guilty surge of gratitude that it wasn't their turn to die. It wasn't only over the target that the flak claimed victims; in some places the proximity of several cities caused the defensive zones to overlap. In this way, the Ruhr in particular and to a lesser extent the Frankfurt – Mainz – Mannheim area, became huge flak and searchlight zones 60 miles across. This was where a good navigator proved his worth by keeping his aircraft in the bomber stream. The heavy calibre guns, especially when radar predicted and engaging single bombers, could be deadly accurate.

Mid-air collisions were also exacting an ever-increasing toll. Routes to targets could have many turning points to keep the Germans guessing until the last moment where to send their fighters. These were often in thick cloud, which could be very hairy indeed. Many times a black shape loomed out of the darkness and mist at those points just missing us. Also, back at the bomber bases many collisions occurred when tired pilots had relaxed their vigilance when circling waiting for their turn to land.

It was true that I minimised the threat of the night fighter, for I was sure that if we saw him first and the gunners gave me, 'Corkscrew port or starboard go' at the correct range, I could lose him and he would go away and find an easier target. As mentioned earlier, however, we knew nothing at the time of the deadly *Schrage Musik*.

* * * * *

I had great faith in the corkscrew evasion tactic with an orthodox fighter attack. We practised it a lot with the Spitfires from Digby. If the gunners waited until the fighter was at a range of between 400 and 600 yards, I always managed to lose him and this was always in daylight; at night it would be easier still. It was a stomach-churning manoeuvre, the gunner who could see the enemy, guiding the pilot who could not. A pilot's confidence in throwing his aircraft through the sky was vital although sometimes I thought I would pull the wings off.

Here then is a typical Lancaster corkscrew for a fighter attacking from the port side. Gunner gives 'Corkscrew port go', pilot then pulls steep bank to port, full left rudder and dive sideways for a thousand feet, wrench the aileron controls to starboard, soar into a climbing turn to the right, then opposite aileron and dive again…The speed varied between 260 and 90mph, the altimeter lost and regained a thousand feet, the rate of descent and ascent varied between 1,000 and 2,000ft a minute, the horizon level just went mad and the rate of turn and skid needles varied from a maximum to port and a maximum to starboard every half minute. The physical exertion for each pull at the bottom of each dive was about equal to pulling on a pair of oars in a boat race.

I firmly believed (although they might have begged to differ!) that the gunners had little chance of shooting down a well-armoured German fighter before he got us with his 20mm and sometimes 30mm cannon and that our only hope of survival therefore lay in escape. Accordingly, I stressed to the gunners that their true value was as lookouts. If they saw the German first, we could survive; if they did not, we were probably dead men.

Our mid-upper gunner, Frank Fathers, was quiet, cool and always alert. I depended on him as the main controller of our defence. We were the same age, height and weight – 22 yrs; 5ft 7½in; 9st 11lb.

I remember, not long after we were crewed up, the six of us being in the Miners' club in Bircotes near Doncaster. The club was crowded and the chairman threw out a challenge to anyone who would care to take on their champion, Dorothy, in downing a pint of beer in the fastest time. Frank immediately put up his hand and was soon alongside the formidable Dorothy, pints at the ready. Dorothy was at least 16 stone, a miner's wife and the quaffer of about 10 pints a night. The steady stream of aircrew from the OTU and volunteers like Frank provided her with plenty of free beer, much to the relief of her husband. As it turned out the result was a dead heat. Both Frank and Dorothy seemed to lock open their throats and the beer gurgled away like buckets of water down a sink; their empty glasses hit the counter as one. The cheers were mostly for Frank as the miners thought that the slim gunner had no chance.

Arthur Clayton the tail-gunner was an entirely different character from Frank. Cheerful, chatty, laid back, his was the loneliest, coldest job in the crew. Tubby, like most tail gunners, removed the central perspex panel in his turret to improve visibility and such were the aerodynamics of the Fraser-Nash design that the slipstream was sucked straight into his face. Sitting for hours in a freezing turret often dulled the mind and reflexes of even the best gunners. So I called him on the intercom more than the rest of the crew and suffered the resultant chatter; at least we knew he was awake! A more medicinal aid to his staying alert was that Tubby sometimes took the strong amphetamines which were available to those aircrew who felt they would be beneficial. This was all very well so long as the night raid went ahead as planned. However, I remember that on more than one occasion, when I was still sharing quarters with my crew and operations were cancelled, Tubby couldn't sleep a wink because he had taken these damn things before the news came through. The rest of us didn't bother with the benzedrenes so we had Tubby chuntering on all night until we threw our boots at him and told him in no uncertain terms to shut up. More polite requests had proved futile as he just retorted: 'Look if I can't get to sleep then I'll make sure you buggers don't either!'

All of the crew smoked fairly heavily apart from myself. My father had virtually chain smoked Woodbine even when in the house and this had put me off taking up smoking for life for which I suppose I should be indirectly thankful to him. I remember it sending a shudder down my spine just hearing the sound of him striking up a match at home. It was particularly unpleasant in winter when the windows would be closed. When I think about it the overwhelming majority of personnel at Wickenby were smokers and if you didn't happen to indulge then passive smoking was just something you had to put up with. Unlike today, the longer term health implications were not something that anyone would have given a moment's thought to, given the rather more immediate risks we faced.

The last three days of January saw more heavy snow showers and aircrews were again set to clearing aircraft, dispersals and runways. Not only that but operations were continually ordered and then cancelled, sometimes even after all engines were running. The two red lights shooting into the sky gave us little satisfaction as we would rather have gone on the operation and got it over with.

Finally on 1 February, after spending all morning shovelling snow, we were briefed for a raid on Ludwigshafen on the Rhine just south of Mannheim. The main targets were the railway yards. Although the snow had stopped falling the weather wasn't good and when the expected red lights did not appear we took off at 4pm.

Climbing in a circle through cloud I settled Roger 2 on a course for Selsey Bill where, at 20,000ft we altered course for the turning point south of Saarbrucken. On this leg I had not engaged the auto-pilot and unusually for me, was chatting to the crew 'aboot naething much ata'. Gus said, 'What are you weaving for Jock?' and I replied, 'I'm not weaving', and prattled on about flying a straighter course than 'George' even. Gus then said, 'Greg, you had better check the skipper's oxygen supply'. The next thing I was aware of was Greg shaking my shoulder saying, 'Jock, you were not connected up', and him slamming in the bayonet fitting of my oxygen tube to the aircraft supply point. I soon recovered but it could have been serious if the autopilot had been in control and had I not been so garrulous, I could easily have lapsed into unconsciousness.

Later, approaching the turning point at Saarbrucken, Gus had given me a slight alteration to course when suddenly, without any warning, the rear turret's guns opened fire and Frank immediately shouted, 'You stupid bastard Tubby, its a Lanc.' The Lancaster had probably been doing an orbit in the stream to lose time (which was frowned on by Bomber Command), and as he came curving into us, Tubby, half-asleep, had panicked and pulled the triggers.

The other Lancaster had then dived to port to avoid the four streams of tracer. Frank thought we must have hit him but 303 bullets would not do much damage unless they hit some of the crew. I refrained from reprimanding our rear gunner, remembering how enthusiastically he had worked that morning on snow clearance and also my own shortcoming in not connecting up my oxygen supply. I resolved there and then to refuse any more snow clearing by our crew before an operation. It was clear that hard manual labour was not conducive to crew efficiency before a seven-hour plus sortie.

On a course of 060 degrees approaching Ludwigshaven we were in thin high layer cloud and Stan asked me to descend. I came down to 15,000ft where Stan saw red TIs well placed above the railway yards and bombed them. The raid appeared to be scattered due to the high layer cloud and the flak was now bursting above us as I turned south then on to a westerly course.

Landing at Wickenby after 11pm and extremely fatigued, I was in a belligerent mood. Before the debriefing the crew heard me utter an oath I hardly ever use when I buttonholed the Flight Commander, Sqd Leader Irving and said, 'We are not going to shovel any more f*****g snow before an op. We are too tired and making uncharacteristic mistakes'. To my surprise he just nodded and walked away.

There was a mystery about Sqn Leader Irving that I have never been able to fathom. He came to our Squadron with his crew at the end of November. He was already a Sqd/Ldr, and got the job of Flight Commander, taking over from Sqd/Ldr Shanley who had finished his tour. It was thought that he had been previously in Training Command before completion of OTU and HCU with his crew. Since his arrival he had not been on any operations but he did go on the Ludwigshaven raid and the very next day was posted to No. 6 Lancaster

Finishing School, leaving his crew at Wickenby. Exactly one month later we were to get his navigator F/O Good when Gus finished his second tour. More about that later but we were never to know the full story concerning his sudden departure.

Next day after a late afternoon briefing we took off at 8.30pm on Bomber Command's one and only large raid on Wiesbaden. There was complete and heavy cloud cover, so much so that the Pathfinders could not mark the target. Bomb aimers had to rely on their navigators giving them 'bombs away' from the picture on their H2S radar screens. Most of the bombing hit the town, destroying the railway station. This was acknowledged by Bomber Command HQ as a great effort by No. 1 Group. That same night 5 Group sent 250 Lancasters to Karlsruhe and the raid was a complete failure. 4 and 6 Groups sent 270 Halifaxes to Wanne-Eickel and that also was a waste of bombs. Twenty-one bombers were lost that night including one from our Squadron piloted by F/Lt Grindrod. It was reported later that he and three of his crew managed to bale out after a mid-air collision with another Lancaster.

It was after 4am before we got to bed and we met at the Flight Office before lunch. Ops were on but only 10 aircraft were required and our crew was not listed. Stan disappeared and when we saw him next he was the owner of a 250cc motorcycle. It was an Excelsior two stroke and he paid £10 for it. He bought it from another Australian who had finished his tour and was going home.

Next day 4 February, no operations were ordered and the Squadron was given a rare stand down. It must have been a Saturday because Stan and I, as rear pillion passenger, travelled the 40 miles to Doncaster and attended the greyhound racing meeting that night. I can't remember whether we won or lost, but the trip home I certainly won't forget. We had no lights, the roads were icy and the wind from the East was freezing cold. There we were with peaked caps back to front, roaring along into the teeth of the wind. When we got back to Wickenby I was like a block of ice and I had been sheltered by Stan's bulk. Who said Australians could not stand the cold?

* * * * *

After Sqd/Ldr Irving's sudden departure F/Lt Lane was promoted to Flight Commander and given the rank of Sqd/Ldr. In Bomber Command, officers on operational duties were one step up in rank and pay and therefore a Squadron Leader commanded a Flight, and a Wing Commander a Squadron. When I got my commission I went straight to Flying Officer skipping Flight Sgt, Warrant Officer and Pilot Officer, a jump of four ranks.

The morning after the stand down, Sqd/Ldr Lane and I were first to arrive at the flight office. Eager to do well in his new post, he put me on a fighter affiliation detail. The weather looked ropy but I assumed he had just come from the Met office and that it would improve. It was also his responsibility to organise the rendezvous with the Spitfire. Getting my crew together we were soon airborne in Roger 2 and waiting in the area for the fighter to bounce us. We were at 18,000ft having climbed through thick cloud all the way when I received a message from Control diverting us to Acklington, north of Newcastle. The weather had rapidly deteriorated with cloud base at 250ft and visibility at 200yd and getting worse.

I was fed up with diversions; hanging about on a strange aerodrome with only flying gear on waiting for the weather to clear was a bind. It wouldn't have been so bad if a few other crews were with us, as a good poker game is a great time passer. I called our Controller and checked wind direction and barometric pressure and asked for the airfield lights to be put on as I was coming in.

Letting down over the sea, we broke cloud at only 200ft in heavy rain a few miles off Grimsby. I could not see ahead so dropped down to 50ft and looked obliquely down through the port window at the white-capped waves and turned west. Passing over Spur Head then roaring over the north Grimsby suburbs I spotted the Grimsby – Lincoln railway line and followed that round. Calling Control I informed them we would be landing on runway 210 in three minutes. Lowering 20 degrees of flap and the undercarriage, I strained to see the small town of Market Rasen. As the spire of the church appeared I broke away port from the railway line then hard starboard across the racecourse. I cut the throttles while still on the turn and, curving on to the runway, straightened up making a pretty good three point landing. The control tower was not visible so I informed them we were down and making for dispersal.

I think we were the only aircraft flying from a Lincolnshire airfield that day and certainly the only Lancaster up from Wickenby. I heard nothing further from Control for disobeying the diversion instruction but my head would certainly have been on the block if I had damaged the aircraft in landing. Sqd/Ldr Lane apologised to me for not checking with Met first. He later turned out to be a first class Flight Commander.

* * * * *

The bad weather continued until 7 February when we were briefed for a night raid on Kleve. This operation was to prepare the way for the attack of the 15 (Scottish) Division across the German frontier near Reichswald. The Germans had included the towns of Goch and Kleve in their strong defences here. The Halifaxes of 4 Group were to attack Goch. It was understood that the civilian populations had been evacuated.

We took off at 7pm and at 10pm were approaching the target on a heading of 060 degrees at 10,000ft. There was a layer of thin cloud at 5,000ft and we clearly heard the Master Bomber ordering the main force to come below cloud. The MB was Wing Commander (Tubby) Baker who was in a Lancaster circling wide round Kleve at 3,000ft. (I had originally wrongly assumed he was in a Mosquito which was the aircraft normally flown by the MB.)

To comply with the order I closed the throttles and put Roger 2 into a dive, getting under the cloud and levelling off at 4,000ft. This turned out to be one hell of a bombing run. Over half of the main force did not come below cloud and bombed the fires and flares, which could be seen through the thin layer.

The 140 or so Lancasters who did obey the MB converged on to the tight bunch of target indicators. Stan gave 'bomb doors open', then came the clear casual voice of the Master Bomber, 'Bomb to the starboard of the red TIs'. I then had to dodge under a Lancaster coming from our port side. Looking up into his yawning bomb bay with its rows of 500lb bombs and cookie, I jabbed left rudder to clear him. Stan who could not see the other Lancaster, had started his run up patter giving me 'right', shouted agitatedly, ' right, right, not bloody left'.

The scene ahead was fantastic; red and yellow tracer shells were cris crossing from the flak batteries outside the town. They seemed to be coming from eight different positions and looked like 20mm and 37mm, which are nasty blighters at the height we were at. Strings of bombs were coming through the cloud from the Lancasters above. Flashes from the exploding blockbusters on the ground were blinding. A stricken Lancaster crashed on its run in, blowing up with its full bomb load. Large columns of black smoke were rising from the town to 3,000ft.

Stan gave 'right, right, steady, bombs away', then Roger 2 was bucking and rearing as the pressure waves hit us; 4,000ft was reckoned to be the absolute minimum height for dropping blockbusters. At last we were through the target and turning south over the Rhine where my stomach muscles started to relax.

At the debriefing after 1am, crews who had bombed from 10,000ft were reporting a quiet trip with no opposition, while those of us who were under the cloud gave lurid descriptions of near collisions, 'friendly' bombs passing close and light flak guns hosing streams of multi-coloured tracer shells.

Frank said that a string of bombs with a wobbling blockbuster dropped past within a few feet of our starboard tail plane as our own bombs were leaving. Tubby made us all laugh when he said he had his hands over his head and was shitting himself.

We heard later that Lieutenant General Brian Horrocks, the Corps Commander in charge of the ground attack, claimed that he had requested an incendiary raid but Bomber Command dropped over a thousand tons of high explosive on the town and no incendiaries. The attack ground to a halt because of the ruins which blocked their way through Kleve.

Few details on casualties and damage were later available from local reports. However, after the war, Kleve claimed to be the most completely destroyed town in Germany of its size.

Richard Dimbleby, the celebrated broadcaster and presenter, made a recording from the cockpit of a 153 Squadron Lancaster from Scampton piloted by John Gee during the attack on Kleve. I have a copy of this recording which was broadcast on the BBC's Radio Newsreel programme. In the broadcast, Dimbleby describes how the Master Bomber ordered the force of 295 Lancasters to bomb below the 10/10 cloud cover. It is a brief but dramatic recording and it is obvious that the aircraft Dimbleby was on was having a pretty rough time of it. It is also clear from his and John Gee's subsequent account of the raid that their aircraft was certainly one of those which did comply with the MB's instruction! I cannot help but admire Dimbleby's courage and dedication to his calling in going on such an operation (he also made another recording during a raid on Berlin). He must have been well aware of the high level of risk this entailed and that, for example, on the Munich raid the previous month over 2 per cent of the bombers involved had been lost. Dimbleby was later the first reporter to go inside the Belsen concentration camp and the first war correspondent from the west to enter the ruined city of Berlin.

For the next three days, operations were ordered then cancelled, usually before 6pm. There were some great games of poker in the mess. It was always dealer's choice with the Canadians favouring 'fours, whores and one eyed jacks' and 'baseball' while the Aussies went for 'spit in the ocean' and 'double fiery cross'. I can't remember having any great wins; I was just happy to have all my good luck in the air over Germany.

CHAPTER 14
DRESDEN

On Tuesday 13 February 1945, we had been detailed for a practice bombing and air testing of a new Lancaster, T – Tommy 2 in the forenoon. On returning to the Flight Office about noon we saw that our names were on the battle order for that night in our own Roger 2. After lunch we went down to dispersal to find the Lancasters were being given the maximum load of fuel, which meant a deep penetration raid.

At the pre-flight meal everyone was trying to guess where the target would be. Gus said, 'Berlin maybe, Butch hasn't sent anyone there for a while'. I didn't fancy that – earlier in my tour perhaps but this was to be my 26th op and survival was uppermost in my mind. I would be glad to miss out on the 'big city'.

Gus and I walked to the briefing room where on the wall map a long red ribbon began in Lincolnshire, dived down to Reading, went south and east over France, then south of Cologne, past Stuttgart then north east between Frankfurt and Mannheim before moving in the direction of Nuremberg, over unknown towns in the province of Saxony to a place called Dobeln, from where there was a 40 mile run in to the target – DRESDEN.

Nobody had ever heard of Dresden being raided before and we thought it a safe bet that it would not be heavily defended like the Ruhr cities or Berlin. I felt almost cheerful until the portent of the briefing sunk in.

Once the main briefing began, talk hushed to silence as crews sat squeezed on benches in front of tables covered in maps. Until recently, we were told, Dresden had been relatively unimportant but since the recent advance of Russian troops it was a vital communications and supply centre for the eastern front. The population would be swollen with German troops and refugees. Up to 800 Lancasters would be operating and the attack was to be in two phases, with our Squadron due to reach the target at the start of the second phase which was timed for 1.30am. A Master Bomber would be present over the target area radioing instructions to bomb aimers. We were also told that, although cloud lay over much of the continent, the sky would be clear over Dresden.

During the briefing I remembered newsreels taken early in the war of long streams of refugees, their possessions piled on handcarts and prams, scattering in panic as bombs fell from Stuka dive-bombers. The memory was instant and vivid and left me feeling disturbed, and the recollection of that moment of memory is itself so vivid that it has never left me.

When briefing had finished I collected the escape kits and distributed them to the crew while we waited for the bus to take us to Roger 2's dispersal. It seemed they were all a little tense. This was to be the longest trip we had ever flown and would take us to within 60 miles of the advancing Russians. It would mean we would be in the air for about 10 hours.

We took off at 21:23 hours; the leaders of the first wave would now be on the last lap of their flight to Dresden. I trimmed the aircraft and put the automatic pilot on for the flight across England.

The night was dark but starlight was strong enough to throw the English coastline into relief. I put Roger 2 into a climb and ordered the crew to switch on their oxygen. By the time I had switched on the 'S' gear we were over France. Cloud had formed and a vast whiteness lay below.

Gus said we were passing over the battle lines and shortly afterwards that, 'Jerry's jamming Gee'. A long silence followed as Roger 2 droned into the night.

Don spoke suddenly, 'Flak to starboard' and I said, 'Some on the port too'. Gus said, 'That's right we are between Frankfurt and Mannheim and you should see Nuremberg's defences opening up soon on our starboard'. I asked Tubby if he was still awake and he answered, 'Not half, I'm bloody cold, this electric suit isn't working'.

At Dobeln we turned starboard and started the run in to the target and, although we were 40 miles from Dresden, fires were reddening the sky ahead. The Met forecast had been correct and there was no cloud over the city.

Ten miles from the target other Lancasters were clearly visible, their silhouettes black in the rosy glow. The streets of the city were a fantastic latticework of fire; blazing streets stretched from east to west, from north to south, in a gigantic saturation of flame.

There was no flak or searchlights over the target and no evidence of any fighters. Stan bombed the centre of the built up area on the southern edge of the fires. We did not hear the Master Bomber until well after our bombs were away and we had started to move out of the target area. It transpired later that, due to the extraordinary success of 5 Group's (the first wave) marking and bombing, an urgent discussion had taken place at this point between the Master Bomber, the Canadian Squadron Leader, C.P.C. De Wesselow, and his chief marker, Wing Commander Le Good, as they hovered at around 8,000ft over the city. The issue was whether they should instruct the bombers to drop into the existing area of fires, thus probably uselessly duplicating the destruction, or to extend the bombing over the other areas of the city outside the districts already attacked. Apparently it was decided, in an *ad hoc* decision, to move the attack into new territory.

After the target Gus gave me a course to pass Nuremberg on its other side from our outward track. As we bored into the night I had time to reflect. To me this seemed to have been an undefended city full of refugees, although undoubtedly there had been a large number of German army units and supplies as well. I felt uneasy and sad.

Time then dragged by and I saw flak spurting up ahead and in the distance searchlights coning a luckless Lancaster. The number of searchlights and flak indicated a large town and Gus confirmed that it was Nuremberg. Frank in the mid upper turret moaned, ' Are we not past there yet; how many more miles to the Gerry border?' Gus replied, 'A couple of hundred miles'.

A stream of red tracer curled ahead showing that enemy fighters must be nearby. Stan stood up into the front gun turret and checked his guns were on 'fire'. Fighter flares lobbed down in front like big slow falling stars and we knew that the enemy was prowling somewhere above. The flares drifted behind and disappeared and Gus said eventually that we had passed the battle lines.

The first weak light of day was lighting the sky behind us when we crossed the French coast. We touched down at base nine hours and 35 minutes after take-off, having covered approximately 1,900 miles.

All squadron aircraft returned safely and at interrogation crews spoke among themselves about the vast conflagration. Nobody had seen anything to compare with Dresden. Measurements and talk of a fantastic glow in the sky did not describe acre upon acre of streets ravaged by fire typhoons and the enormous bowl of rosy light that reached to altitudes unattainable by aircraft.

Subsequently, of course, the raids on Dresden over 13/14 February 1945 gained particular notoriety. By the morning of the 14th, 796 RAF Lancasters and 311 US AAF Flying Fortresses had dropped more than 4,500 tons of high explosives and incendiary devices. At least 25,000 inhabitants (possibly many more) had perished in the terrible firestorm and 13 square miles of the city's historic centre, including incalculable quantities of treasure and works of art, lay in ruins.

* * * * *

We got to bed after 9am, immediately after breakfast. I slept for four hours then washed, shaved and dressed. I was looking forward to having a night out and a few pints of beer but thought that I'd better make certain at the Flight Office that our crew would not be required that night. 'Nothing on?' I said to a sergeant standing at the door. 'There is', he said, 'a battle order has just gone up for tonight.' A paper was pinned to the notice board which contained a typewritten list of names which included our crew. Briefing was at 4pm. I then carried on to the crew hut to make sure they were awake and to impart the happy news!

At the briefing 12 crews were listed, nine of which were to bomb Chemnitz with the main force, while three crews were to lay mines in the Kadet Channel between the Danish island of Falster and the German seaport of Rostock. We had been detailed for the minelaying sortie and Roger 2 had been loaded with six Mk VI mines each weighing 2,000lb. In addition to minelaying, the force of 24 Lancasters and 24 Halifaxes were to carry out a spoof raid on Berlin as part of an elaborate diversion plan to draw off the German fighters from the main force attacking Chemnitz later (48 bombers dropping Window can look a formidable force on the German radar screens).

On the huge wall map there were two red-ribboned routes. One for the main raid to Chemnitz, about 200 miles south of Berlin. This force would consist of 500 Lancasters and 200 Halifaxes. The other was for the small minelaying force. Our route entailed a long run across the North Sea, crossing over Denmark north of Kiel, then skirting the island of Lolland before the red ribbon reached Falster. Here we would be fewer than 100 miles from neutral Sweden. A sharp turn to the south-east would then take us towards the German mainland just east of Rostock. At a designated point on this leg the mines would be dropped on their parachutes at three-second intervals. Carrying on this course we would then cross the German coast heading for Berlin. Sixty miles from Berlin at a place called Neustrelitz, we turned west taking us between Hamburg and Bremen.

We took off at 6pm and set course for Denmark, keeping below 1,000ft to avoid the German radar picking us up too quickly. The seemingly endless sea journey became monotonous. We were the only moving thing except for the occasional falling star. The sea below us was horribly black. Eventually, crossing the enemy coast, I put Roger 2 into a climb to reach the mine-dropping altitude of 10,000ft.

Crossing over Denmark we reached the island of Falster where Gus gave me a course for Berlin. We were soon in the mine release area and I opened the bomb doors. Stan activated the timing release when Gus gave the signal. It was a relief to feel the mines drop off one by one and get the bomb doors closed.

As we approached the German coast, cloud formed below. Frank reported a combat well astern of us, but he could not see the aircraft involved, just the tracer arcs. My thoughts at that moment were of the German night fighters gathering to defend Berlin and hoping they would not come to meet us before we turned away.

It was a strange, tense situation with six pairs of eyes searching the darkness diligently, hoping to see nothing. After what seemed an age, Gus gave me a course of 265 degrees but I was aware that this would track us over the German night fighter airfields of Parchim and Stade. Later, passing midway between Bremen and Hamburg, their defences were not activated and at long last Gus informed us that we were passing over the Frisian Islands. Don fished out the coffee flask and poured me a cup – the swill tasted lovely.

At the debriefing the three minelayers reported a quiet trip with no opposition. Later though we found out that five Halifaxes and two Lancasters had been shot down by German night fighters out of the 48 in the mine laying force. A total of 24 heavy bombers were lost during the night's operations.

We had completed six weeks of operations and were granted a week's leave. Stan, Greg and I went to Aberdeen where the Australians again enjoyed the hospitality of the Caledonian Hotel, thanks to Lord Nuffield.

On our return to Wickenby we learned that four complete crews had been killed during our absence. All were experienced and had done 20 or more missions. Two of them, under F/O Lucas and F/O Holloway, were the only losses suffered by Bomber Command on 18 February when a small force of Lancasters laid mines in the German Bight. F/O Paterson and crew had been killed over Dortmund and F/O Rodger and crew were lost over Duisburg the very next day, 21 February. We knew all of them well having been at the same HCU together. Harold Lucas and Donald Rodger and their crews had spent the night at Charter Hall with us after having been diverted there following the mine laying sortie on 14 January. To add to our gloom, Gus had now completed 23 operations with us and was deemed to have finished his second tour. For all of those missions his navigation had been faultless, we had always been in the middle of the bomber stream and also spot on time at the targets. We all felt keenly that he would be sorely missed and, although at that point we thought we only had four more ops to complete our tour, a directive then came through from Butch Harris increasing a tour of operations to 36. The unusually bad weather over the winter had bottlenecked the OTUs and there were not enough new crews coming through to replace tour expired types and crews lost through enemy action. Gus was deservedly out of it but the rest of us still had some way to go.

* * * * *

On 28 February we were briefed and then took off for a daylight raid on the rail marshalling yards at Neuss. We had another engineer with us as Don's wife had given birth to a daughter a few days before and he was delayed in returning from leave. He was actually walking from the local railway station at Snelland when he saw the Squadron take off. Never having missed an op with the crew, he was really downhearted. As it happened we got an early recall and landed just two and quarter hours later. He wasn't so pleased though when he found out that we had to do six extra operations. I could see it was weighing heavily on his mind but after no doubt some inner torment he manfully accepted the situation. Don Leader was conscientious, cool and courageous and there were many occasions when I was glad that this steady character was beside me in the cockpit.

The cancellation of the raid on Neuss meant that we returned with full bomb loads including the thin-skinned 4,000lb blockbuster. It was considered too dangerous to land with a cookie so the Squadron was ordered to fly out over the North Sea and jettison them. There was scattered cloud at 5,000ft in the dropping zone and as I wished to see the waterspout from the explosion, I had Lancaster X-Ray 2 under the cloud when Stan dropped the bomb. As the bomb left I banked hard to port and looking down saw a small fishing boat right in the middle of three huge waterspouts. It must have been a restricted area and he obviously should not have been there. He was not harmed but I bet he steered clear of that area from then on.

As previously mentioned, another navigator joined the crew to replace Gus Marbaix. F/O Al Good, a Canadian, was round faced, of medium height and placid with a perpetual smile. During forthcoming operations we would often be out of the bomber stream and getting more than our share of predicted flak, but at least Al would sound calm and unruffled through it all. I don't recall him ever once coming out of his cabin to see the fireworks outside.

Heavy calibre flak, when radar predicted and engaging single aircraft, could be deadly accurate. If a lone bomber did not know he was being tracked and remained on a steady course, a crack German flak battery would normally down him with three shells. The first shell was a marker and you would be unlucky to be hit by it, but the following ones would be close enough for the kill. Not all flak was near the German cities. Perhaps the most effective flak were the special mobile batteries of heavy guns mounted on railway trucks which could appear unexpectedly at places not marked on the bomber crews' flak maps.

About noon on 1 March we took off to raid Mannheim. After an hour or so I could see we were well out of the bomber stream but said nothing. A navigator must be given his head and on a night raid I probably would not have been able to tell if we were out of the stream or not. On the last leg to the target I estimated that we were still 10 miles off track to the left of the bomber stream when Frank reported a single flak burst 200 yards astern and at our height. I turned starboard 20 degrees. The next burst was close to where we would have been and the third shell would have blown us out of the sky if we had not changed course.

We were now converging on to the stream as the flak barrage over Mannheim started. There was $^{10}/_{10}$ths cloud at 12,000ft and we were at 17,000ft. The Pathfinder Mosquitoes had marked the aiming point with blue smoke puffs and on the Master Bomber's instructions, Stan bombed the starboard one of two of them. At the debriefing at 6.30pm we had voiced the criticism that blue smoke puffs looked similar to flak bursts until close on the bombing run.

The next day after an early briefing we were airborne at 7am to bomb Cologne. Crossing the German border before 10am we had clear skies and good visibility. Again we were out of the stream, on the starboard this time, when Frank reported a single flak burst astern. Turning 40 degrees to port I reckoned that the next two shells would have got us if we had carried on the same course. Stan then took over, 'Right, bomb doors open, right.' We were now in among the other Lancasters and Halifaxes, and ahead lay the vast sprawl of Cologne. The Master Bomber gave 'Pickwick', the code word for pick your own spot. Even at 17,000ft, the magnificent cathedral could be clearly seen towering above the bomb smoke. It was more of a plea than an order when I said, 'Don't go near the cathedral Stan'. Three Lancasters were hit by flak and went down in flames. One of them crashed into a large bridge over the Rhine and as to whether it was a last courageous act by a wounded pilot or just chance, we will never know.

Next thing we were into a hailstorm of flak with one burst close on our port rattling the fuselage with fragments. Stan bombed an area of factory buildings south east of the cathedral.

When well on the way on the homeward leg I asked Frank to check on the damage. He reported many holes between his turret and the tail and a lot of the shrapnel had passed through both sides of the fuselage. After landing at 12.30pm, we examined the scars and found that apart from the fuselage holes, the port rudder was riddled. Tubby was very lucky not to have been seriously wounded or killed. This was the last RAF raid on Cologne, which was captured by American troops four days later.

The following day only five crews were required to lay mines in Oslo fjord and we got an early stand down. I went into Lincoln and met Frank in the Saracen's Head, from there we did a pub-crawl, finishing up in the Assembly Rooms dance hall. Around midnight we were travelling back to Wickenby by taxi with two other aircrew when suddenly all hell broke loose. I heard the bang, bang, bang of cannon shells bursting, then the taxi driver turned hard left into a ditch and we all piled on top of each other.

This was the night that the Luftwaffe mounted their operation 'Gisella', sending over 200 night fighters to follow the various bomber forces back to

England. The move took the British defences by surprise. Bomber Command admitted to over 20 losses inflicted by the Luftwaffe intruders but these losses were aircraft returning from attacking assigned targets in Germany. The record appears not to include a very significant number of aircraft out at the same time on training sorties – three from Wickenby alone. It is probable that total bomber losses topped 60, if the losses on these latter sorties were also to be included.

The German fighters were also shooting up everything that moved around the airfields, which included our taxi. Frank said, 'I don't mind getting shot up over Cologne, but this is my night off!' As it happened our taxi escaped being hit but the ditch was too deep for us to extricate it. We were only a mile from our quarters and as we walked back aircraft were buzzing around with tracer shells arcing overhead. Three of the German fighters (Ju 88s) crashed through flying too low.

The three Lancasters from Wickenby (two from 12 Squadron and one from ours) were new crews on training exercises and were shot down near Horncastle as they approached base; 4 Group suffered most, losing 14 Halifaxes as they were landing with all their crews being killed. The German fighter which crashed near Elvington airfield was the last Luftwaffe aircraft to crash on English soil during the war.

Chapter 15
'I AM ENGLISH'

By Monday 5 March, the training bottleneck had eased and new crews were arriving on the Squadron. On the battle order for that night's operation we had been allocated a second dickey, P/O Fanner. We knew it would be a long haul because each Lancaster had been fuelled up to the brim with 2,154 gallons. I walked to the briefing with our navigator. This would be his first night raid with us and I had not been over impressed with his navigational skills so far. I said to him. 'You'd better keep your finger out tonight Al, it looks like we will be a long time over Germany.' He just widened his smile and gave a slight nod of the head.

We settled down at our table and I noted that the target was Chemnitz, 35 miles east of Leipzig. The Met man gave his briefing, warning us of severe icing conditions, then the Senior Intelligence Officer took the stand. He informed us we were part of a 700 Lancaster and Halifax force to continue operation 'Thunderclap'. At the Yalta conference on 4 February, the Russians had asked for attacks on German cities near the eastern front. (After the war they renamed Chemnitz, Karl Marx Stadt.)

The SIO continued, 'To help those of you who might be so unfortunate to have to bale out and make for the battle lines of our well beloved, but notoriously trigger happy, Russian allies, The Air Ministry have come up with these'. Orderlies then came round issuing each crew member with a folder containing a Union Jack printed on a silk-like material with words in Russian. The translation: 'I am English, please communicate my particulars to the British Military Mission, Moscow.' On the other side:

INSTRUCTIONS

1. Learn by heart the Russian phrase 'Ya Anglichanin' (Means 'I am English' and is pronounced as spelt).
2. Carry this folder and contents in left breast pocket.
3. If you have time before contact with Russian troops take out folder and attach it (flag side outwards) to front of pocket.
4. When spotted by Russian troops put up your hands holding the flag in one of them and call out the Phrase 'Ya Anglichanin'.
5. If you are spotted before taking action as at para.3. do NOT attempt to extract folder or flag. Put up your hands and call out the phrase – 'Ya Anglichanin'. The folder will be found when you are searched.
6. You must understand that these recognition aids CANNOT be accepted by Soviet troops as proof of bona fides as they may be copied by the enemy. They should however protect you until you are cross-questioned by competent Officers.

As we read the instructions the ribald comments started. One burly Canadian gunner could not contain himself and in a loud voice queried,' I am English?' The SIO smiling, said, 'If the Canadians, Australians, New Zealanders, Scots, Irish and Welsh object, they can find out the Russian translation for their various nationalities and swot that up before take-off…or they can walk the 500 miles or so West to our own battle lines'.

Needless to say, we were all a bit tight lipped about the bland optimism of our staff brothers at Air Ministry. Even if the Russians held their fire as we walked over 'no mans land', waving our wee Union Jacks, the Germans certainly would not.

At 4.30pm, Blondie the WAAF driver dropped us off at X-Ray 2's dispersal. The light had faded and light drizzle was falling as the ground crew loaded the last packets of Window, into the nose compartment.

On the subject of Window I was to have the privilege many years later of meeting up with Professor Reginald Victor Jones, the physicist and scientific military intelligence expert who played an important role in the defence of Britain in World War Two. Reg Jones was largely instrumental in the devising and later deployment of Window among many other achievements, and his autobiography, *Most Secret war; British Scientific Intelligence* 1939–1945, formed the basis of the BBC One TV documentary series, *The Secret War,* first aired in January 1977. I was fortunate to be able to spend quite some time with him at his home in Aberdeen and was utterly fascinated by what he had to say. For his part he seemed genuinely interested to hear of my experiences of flying a Lancaster in operations.

Apart from dealing with Window, it was also the bomb aimer's job to empty the syrup tin used by the pilot out of the same chute. The pilot on a Lancaster was the only one of the crew who could not leave his station and use the 'Elsan' toilet near the tail of the aircraft. Usually on the outward journey of an op I needed to use the can frequently, so the call, 'Pass the can Stan' was a familiar request.

Waving chocks away at 4.45pm and taxiing round to the runway, the sky was now clear and I could see that the moisture on the wings had started to freeze and had a coating of white. It seemed the take-off run took much longer and I had to keep the nose down until well away from the airfield before the speed built up. We learned later that 10 Halifaxes from 6 Group crashed soon after take-off due to icy conditions. One of the Halifaxes crashed in the city of York killing several civilians. Over 30 more heavy bombers would be shot down on this raid and another raid the same night on the synthetic-oil refinery at Bohlen, making it an expensive night for Bomber Command.

Approaching the German border between Saarbrucken and Luxembourg, I put X-Ray 2 into a climb to our bombing altitude of 16,000ft and Stan started to push out the Window. Climbing past 12,000ft I had just engaged the superchargers when over the intercom Stan burst out laughing and said, 'I'm sorry Jock, your piss tin has abandoned ship'. Most of the crew then pressed their mike switches so that I could hear their chuckles.

Now at 16,000ft and feinting towards Frankfurt, I was about to ask P/O Fanner to take over while I went back to the elsan when Frank reported a flak burst 150 yards astern. I immediately turned starboard 20 degrees and sure enough, two further explosions occurred near enough where we would have been. Turning port 40 degrees then resuming our original course, I thought, 'Bloody hell we are out of the stream again!'

All thoughts of letting Bill Fanner take over were abandoned but I was really bursting now. I said, 'Stan, you have got to find something for me to use as a piss tin, and stop Windowing'. If a bomber is out on his own, his Window trail shows him up more prominently on the German radar screens.

I then said to Al, ' It looks like we are out of the stream. Do you reckon it's port or starboard?' He just got out, 'Starboard, the wind is stronger than forecast', when Frank and Tubby both shouted a warning about another flak burst close astern and spot on our height. I turned 20 port and climbed a thousand feet. I could see the following flak bursts out of the starboard window and said, 'I will keep on this course Al until you think we are back in the stream' and, 'Stan if you can't find anything I'll have to piss out of the port window and as it's 50 below zero outside I don't want a frost-bitten willie'.

Stan then unhitched one of the ammo cans from the front gun turret, which received the spent cartridge cases, and handed it up to me. Frank then said, 'Flak burst 100 yards astern, low'. Turning starboard 20, I had the ammo can awkwardly between my legs and did the needful. As I watched the two following flak bursts off to port I felt hot liquid running into my left flying boot then remembered that there was a slit in the bottom corner of ammo cans. As I handed the can to Fanner to give to Stan, I said, 'there's damn all in it, it's all gone into my flying boot'. The resulting cackles from the crew at least relieved the tension.

We were now on a course for a feint to Leipzig and below us at 12,000ft, cloud covered Germany. I had asked Stan to try and get fixes from the H2S set to help Al. I knew we must keep in the stream as there was evidence of fighter activity as well. I had seen what looked like two bombers exploding well ahead.

At a place called Zeitz, 25 miles south-west of Leipzig, we turned on to a course of 155 degrees for the target, 40 miles away. Stan squeezed past Don and Fanner and hurriedly checked his bombsight and fusing switch panel.

I felt something strange with my left foot and thought; 'surely it would not freeze up inside a fur lined flying boot'. Just then, spot on zero hour, red and green sky markers burst ahead. Nothing was heard from the Master Bomber and I wondered if he had been shot down. Stan gave me directions and bombed on the centre of three red and green sky markers, giving a 12-second overshoot. We were now in the thick of the flak barrage but I had to keep straight for the photograph. Even though thick cloud covered Chemnitz, the photos could be checked against the pattern of the Pathfinder's flares. I turned starboard on a course which should take us between Nuremberg and Wurzburg. Stan went back on the H2S set to help Al.

By now my foot was numb and I was stamping it on the floor. Engaging the autopilot I took off my flying boot and was surprised to feel my sock ice hard. I passed sock and boot back to Greg so that he could heat them up in the hot air vent while Bill Fanner kneaded and pummelled my foot to get the circulation back.

The long drag back to base was accomplished without further incident. We landed well after 2am after a total of nine and a half hours in the air. A few days later we learned that the centre and south of the city suffered severe fire damage. Several important factories were situated in the fire area and the Siegmar factory, which made tank engines, was completely destroyed.

Chemnitz was our 30th operation and should have been the finish of our tour. There were now plenty of new crews on the Squadron but the order from

Harris to make us do extra six ops was not rescinded. Tubby said, 'If we get the chop on one of these extra trips, I'll be furious'. At that time I would have been glad to finish. The world press condemnation of the carnage wreaked by Bomber Command at Dresden left me little or no stomach for bombing German cities.

Before Dresden, although the German propagandists labelled us as *Terrorfleigers*, I believed that whichever city or target we were attacking was of significant industrial, military or communications importance. The Germans could have evacuated their cities of all but essential workers and then there would have been relatively few innocent casualties. This would have imposed an intolerable strain on Germany, which is what the RAF wanted. The Geneva Convention did not forbid the methods used.

It is perhaps significant that in the post-war controversy, the Germans made the least noise themselves. Without real provocation, Hitler had gone to war with most of Europe. The Nazis had systematically sought to exterminate the Jewish race and had declared all Slavic peoples to be sub-humans. The Gestapo had tortured and terrified throughout occupied Europe and countless thousands of innocent men and women had been dragged off to work in German factories as virtual slaves.

Post-war German historians realised that it was the Nazis who had sown the wind and the now dead Hitler, whom they once followed so faithfully, received much of the blame for the retaliation. Here there was only a tiny questioning of the morality of bombing later in the war and that was by religious leaders not politicians. A country fighting for its very existence cannot afford to have strict boundaries of morality in the means by which it saves itself. It is humbug to suggest that the use of bombers was wrong when it was touch and go whether Britain survived at all.

It is small wonder that we bomber men felt baffled and hurt, when after the war our actions were declared to be unworthy. No one would wish to minimise the importance of the valiant and decisive part played by the fighter pilots in the summer of 1940. However, the fact is that whereas in the whole of the Battle of Britain 507 aircrew were killed, Bomber Command lost 545 men killed in one night raid alone. This figure does not include crews killed in accidents back at their bases or men who baled out and were taken prisoners of war. The official number of aircrew killed in Bomber Command was 55,573 and a further 9,784 were shot down and taken prisoner. The average life expectancy was shorter than that of soldiers on the Western Front in World War One and by 1943 only one in six crew members could expect to survive one tour. In the ensuing years, the RAF glorified each anniversary of the Battle of Britain but little was made of the sacrifice by the thousands who had died over the Ruhr, Berlin and the many other heavily defended German cities.

Much has been written and spoken since the war about Harris, about the effectiveness of the Strategic Bomber Offensive and about its morality. History has seen many land and sea battles but the Strategic Bomber Offensive may never be repeated on that scale and will no doubt continue to interest historians for many years.

Bomber Command was not run by a committee or board but effectively by one man, Air Marshal Sir Arthur Harris. Hindsight gives us the ability to judge that Harris made mistakes but it does not in my view give us the right to be over critical. A General might fight three major battles in his lifetime, an Admiral maybe just one. Harris committed almost the whole of his front line force to combat approximately 10 times in each month for three and a quarter years. Many raids that were subsequently successful would never have taken place if Harris had waited for perfect conditions. Certainly he was a warrior to the roots of his soul and he sought to engage and defeat the enemy by every means at his command. It was this quality in him that undoubtedly appealed to Churchill, a like spirit.

I never saw Harris, indeed very few aircrew did, yet we regarded him with rueful but enduring affection. He was ruthless and notoriously impatient of failure or disagreement. The stories of his abrasive encounters with authority were legion. Striding into the Air Ministry one morning, he passed one of the most senior civil servants with a bluff greeting of, 'Morning Abrahams, and what have you done to impede the war effort today?' His dry, cutting, often vulgar wit was legendary throughout the RAF, as was his ill-concealed contempt for the British Army and Royal Navy. He was fond of saying that the army would never understand the value of tanks until they could be modified to 'eat hay and shit'. He also said that there were three things one should never take on a warship – a wheelbarrow, an umbrella and a naval officer.

One day Churchill told Harris that Sir Dudley Pound was deeply concerned about the continued survival of the German battleship *Tirpitz*. Harris retorted, 'Tell the First Sea Lord he need not worry, I'll sink it when I have a spare moment'. One morning the Prime Minister came on the scrambler for details of the previous night's attack. 'I'm sick of these raids on Cologne', growled Churchill testily. 'So are the people of Cologne,' barked Harris.

From his headquarters at High Wycombe poured a stream of orders and memoranda, that clattered down the tele-types to Groups and Stations to launch 7,000 aircrew into the night sky over Germany.

The following morning HQ received back the paper harvest of signals; still damp reconnaissance prints, provisional bomb tonnage figures and bomber losses by which success or failure was measured. Their absolute remoteness from the battlefront has led some historians to compare High Wycombe with the French chateaux from which the generals of World War One directed offensives such as Passchendaele and the Somme, and consequently to liken Harris to Sir Douglas Haig. But those who seek to present him as such, indifferent to casualties, do him an injustice in my opinion. I believe that he was passionately concerned to give every man in his command the best possible chance of survival.

'Bomber Harris', who had once stood so high in the esteem of the British public, failed to be recognised in the distribution of post-war honours. His request that a special Bomber Command campaign medal be awarded to his crews was refused although a similar decoration was given to Fighter Command men who had fought in the Battle of Britain.

Harris then retired unhonoured to obscurity and it was not until eight years later, when Churchill was again Prime Minister, that Harris became a baronet – an honour often awarded to minor politicians for long service.

CHAPTER 16

FAREWELL TO ROGER 2

On 8 March we were on the battle order for a night raid. Since our minelaying trip on 14 February, Roger 2 had been given a major overhaul and had just been returned to the Squadron. S/Ldr Lane asked me to take it up on an air test, combined with a fighter affiliation exercise, and if I was satisfied with its performance to fly it on tonight's operation.

As the Spitfire attacked repeatedly I threw Roger 2 into corkscrew after corkscrew. Although R 2 was as good as she ever was, I knew the Lancaster we had flown on the last four ops, X-Ray 2 with its paddle propellers could grip the air better than Roger's needle point props and could out perform it. After landing I reported to the Flight Commander and stated a preference for X-Ray 2. If the old war-horse had been flesh and blood I would never have deserted her; even so I had a troubled feeling of disloyalty.

That night the target was Kassel, a city situated about 120 miles east of Essen, and the pilot who took Roger 2, a Cuban (yes, Cuban) F/O Moje Enciso-y-Sieglie and crew had to go through a lengthy spell of corkscrewing to shake off the attentions of an over persistent Focke-Wulf 190. This was the last large RAF raid on this city which had several aircraft factories. For our part the trip was relatively uneventful and only one Mosquito was lost from the total of 276 aircraft deployed.

Roger 2 was a MkIII Lancaster and turned up for work on 31 May 1944. It thereafter did 101 operational sorties against the enemy and for good measure, added five operation 'Manna' (food dropping for the starving Dutch) and one operation 'Exodus' (recovery of ex-prisoners of war) before VE-Day arrived. Roger 2 was the only Lancaster on 626 Squadron to ever do a 'ton-up'and thus is featured in Norman Franks' excellent book *TON-UP LANCS* which came out in 2005.

Given the attrition rate of Lancasters in Bomber Command between 1942 and 1945, it was quite exceptional for a Lancaster to complete over 100 operations. Indeed there were only 35 Lancasters that were able to be named in the 'Ton-Up' Club. A total of 7,366 Lancasters were built of which 3,400 were lost on operations and a further 200 plus were destroyed or written-off in crashes. They undertook approximately 156,000 operational sorties and carried over 600,000 tons of bombs.

Some 125,000 aircrew served in Bomber Command in World War Two, of whom no fewer than 73,700 (almost 60 per cent!) became casualties. For a bomber crew to complete a tour of operations they had to carry out a set number of operations against hostile targets. The number varied, but was generally 30, although as I indicated in the preceding chapter we ultimately had to do 36. Accordingly, from these statistics it is not difficult to appreciate that neither the crew or the aeroplane had a particularly good chance of finishing a set number of bombing missions. In the case of the aircraft, when one crew ended a tour (or were lost in another aeroplane) their usual Lancaster would continue to be sent on ops until it was destroyed or damaged beyond repair.

During its hectic life with 626, 32 different crews took Roger 2 into battle. Of these the majority did four or fewer sorties in this durable Lancaster. We did 18 operations during its charmed life century in the skies over Europe. Only one other crew did more, that of Flying Officer R.C. Bennet from Vancouver. They were the first crew to take her over and their logo 'Bennet's

Beavers', painted on by Bob Bennet himself, remained on the port side under the pilot's window for the duration of its life. The motif was of a red-nosed backwoodsman wearing a raccoon hat. On his shoulder he carried an axe on which was perched a small bird. Aft of it began the rows of bombs. The first block was seven rows of 10, red bombs for night and yellow for day ops. A second block was started behind the first.

Roger 2 went into action for the first time four days before D-Day and kept going all the way up to VE-Day on 9 May 1945. During that time Bomber Command lost 2,128 aircraft with over 10,000 aircrew killed in action. Truly, she wore the halo of good luck. Although she was damaged by flak many times, only one rear gunner, F/O C.M. Bursey, received slight injuries after bombing Falaise on 14 August 1944.

The last recorded flight of Roger 2 from Wickenby was on 11 May 1945 when it took 35 ex-prisoners home, piloted by the same F/O Bill Fanner who helped return my foot to life after I had pissed in my boot on the Chemnitz raid! Shortly after, it was flown to 35 MU to stand by. The war in the Far East had yet to be won but it was never called up again and like many of her sisters, she slowly died of inactivity. In August 1947 her body was dissected, but the memories of those who flew in her live on, a never to be forgotten part of 626 Squadron's luminous history.

* * * * *

It was Sunday 11 March as Al and I walked to the briefing room at 9.30am. I was pleased that it was to be a daylight raid but did not like bombing on a Sunday.

Inside the briefing room a red ribbon on the wall map wound into the heart of the Ruhr. We went closer to the map and saw that the target was Essen. Al made no comment but his bland smile disappeared for an instant. We sat at a table and Al began to draw in courses on his Mercator's chart. The briefing room began to fill up and the rest of our crew joined us. Tubby was the only one to give out an oath when he saw the target was Essen.

The Senior IO began, 'This will be the biggest daylight raid by heavy bombers the world has ever seen'. We were told that more than a thousand bombers would drop in the region of 5,000 tons of bombs. The raid would last nearly half an hour and its object was to wipe out the already damaged Krupps factories and to completely dislocate the transport system. A Master Bomber would control the attack and since cloud was anticipated, blue marker flares would be used. H-hour would be 15:00 hours and our Squadron would be in the first wave. At 11.25am I pushed forward the throttles on X-Ray 2 to start the take off run and she went straight and true down the runway.

At the point where the stream crossed the battle lines it might have looked from below as though it was making for Cologne. However, suddenly it veered to the north east and began the run in on Essen which was covered in cloud with the tops between 6,000 and 7,000ft.

Flak began spurting up through the cloud and was bursting too close for comfort. It appeared to be radar predicted so I turned 10 degrees starboard and started to climb. There were no other aircraft near us but I could see four Lancasters high above, obviously way above their ordered bombing heights. Flak was bursting all around now as I resumed our original course and levelled off at 17,000ft.

H-hour was only minutes away and still there were no markers or any word from the MB. Then at one minute after H-Hour, one solitary blue smoke puff burst ahead from an 'Oboe' Mosquito. The Master Bomber immediately came on the air asking first wave aircraft to bomb on it.

Stan gave directions and as the spot of burning blue floated into the orange graticule of his bombsight, he pressed the tit and 12,000lb of bombs ripped away. I could see a string of bombs from one of the Lancs above dropping dead ahead of us as Stan called, 'No hang ups, close bomb doors'. I stuffed the nose down and built up speed. As I turned port and looked back at the target I could see great volumes of black smoke billowing out of the white clouds.

This was the last RAF raid on Essen, which had been attacked many times, though often with disappointing and costly results. This attack was accurate and virtually paralysed the city and surrounding area until the American troops entered the city some time later.

We landed and taxied to dispersal at 5pm. The ground crew then immediately got busy as there was another maximum effort required for the next day.

* * * * *

There were 1,079 aircraft on the Essen raid and 4.661 tons of bombs were dropped on Oboe-directed sky-markers through complete cloud cover. 'Oboe' became the most precise bombing system of the whole war. It was a brilliantly sophisticated variation of the system by which the Germans had bombed England in 1940. An aircraft flew at the end of a beam laid by a ground station, like a conker on a string whirled round a child's head. Its bombs or markers were released at the exact point of intervention with another beam from a second ground station. There was no scope for visual error and the device proved accurate to within 500 yards. Oboe suffered just two limitations: Bomber Command possessed only two sets of ground stations, and could only control a few aircraft over the target. It was therefore necessary to have Pathfinder heavy bombers constantly available to 'back up' the Oboe markers. The second difficulty was more serious: owing to the curvature of the Earth, Oboe beams could only reach aircraft at limited range from their English ground stations. They could get to the Ruhr but not much further.

On the plus side Harris was now equipped with the perfect aircraft to carry Oboe, the twin-engined De Havilland Mosquito, which could mark from 28,000ft to get the utmost range from the device. Mosquito casualties over Germany were negligible, being a fraction of those suffered by the 'heavies'. They were too fast for the German fighters and too high for the flak. I volunteered for a tour on Mosquitos immediately on finishing my tour on Lancasters but was informed that I had to take a rest of at least three months from operations.

Next day at the briefing the Senior IO informed us the target was Dortmund and that it would be an even heavier raid than yesterday's on Essen. In fact, it was the heaviest raid to date and it stood as the record until the end of the war. Taking off at 1pm, it was almost a replica of yesterday's operation except that the Oboe Mosquito dropped a green smoke marker, the flak was not as heavy and the smoke boiling through the cloud was brown and not black.

A British team which investigated the effects of bombing in Dortmund after the war stated that, 'The final…raid stopped production so effectively that it would have been many months before any substantial recovery could have occurred'.

CHAPTER 17
HITLER'S OIL

The Allied High Command had always accepted that the German oil installations should have been one of the top priorities of both the American and RAF bomber forces. How was it then that Bomber Command with its greater lifting capacity had dropped only about two-thirds the total tonnage of bombs dropped by the USSAF on oil targets?

The answer lies in the decisive breakdown of the RAF's internal Command structure which took place in the winter of 1944, when the Chief of Air Staff, Sir Charles Portal, finally showed himself unable to exercise authority over Sir Arthur Harris. The Chief of Air Staff first requested, then demanded, and at last pleaded with Harris to obey the orders that he had been given.

In his reply to Portal, he violently protested the range of demands on his forces and the 'number of cooks now engaged in stirring the broth'. As he saw it the Admiralty and the ball-bearing experts were tunnelling at his resources again.

It is important to stress what was at stake here. No one familiar with the tactical and weather problems could have expected Bomber Command's aircraft to maintain an unbroken offensive against Germany's oil plants – the

Americans failed to do so, despite their total commitment to the policy. Throughout the winter, the Allied armies had their own urgent and almost compulsory demands on the strategic bomber force. There were targets to be attacked at the behest of the Admiralty, alarmed by the late resurgence in U-boat activity, and also at the urging of the politicians with their own preoccupations. Air Chief Marshall Sir Arthur Tedder himself, Eisenhower's deputy commander, had pressed for the concentrated Battle of the Ruhr in October 1944 – the 'Hurricane' plan. Nonetheless, having made allowances for all these elements, there were still many mornings when Harris sat at his desk confronted with the long list of targets of every kind, together with a weather forecast that – as usual throughout the war – made the C-in-C's decision a matter of the most open judgement. Again and again though, Harris came down in favour of attacking an industrial city rather than oil plants. It appears that he sincerely believed that the use of massed bomber forces against oil installations was a waste of available effort.

Nevertheless, Bomber Command did attack oil installations with an overall total of 94,000 tons of bombs. On 13 March 14 crews including ours were briefed to attack the Dahlbusch benzol plant at Gelsenkirchen. At 5.30pm, with all four engines running, I was about to wave chocks away when the Wingco's car screeched to a halt, he jumped out and beckoned for me to cut the engines. At the last minute he had received a message from Group to reduce the squadron force to 11.

I was cheesed off because this should have been a comparatively easy target and a short five and a half-hour sortie. Back at the locker room I said, 'I am going to Scunthorpe for a damn good booze up, anyone coming with me?'

Stan, Greg, Frank and I made it to Scunthorpe. Starting off at the Bluebell Inn, an old world pub with excellent beer, then on to the Oswald where they had a trio of musicians playing popular songs of the period and where anyone could get up on the stage and sing. The leader of the band was not averse to cutting off, in mid song, any chancer who offended his ear.

We usually finished up in the Crosby Hotel if there was a dance on there. A spiral staircase connected the dance hall with the bar downstairs. With a nice crowd of girls upstairs and good beer downstairs, the stairs were well worn with bods corkscrewing both ways.

We had got to know Scunthorpe the previous summer when we were at Blyton converting to four engine bombers.

In the spring of 1944, the Station medical staff at Blyton, the home of 1662 HCU, faced a new problem in trying to keep as many men flying as possible – VD. There was usually a case or two on most airfields but in April six airmen reported sick at Blyton. It was evidently a serious problem. Through some vigorous questioning, it seemed that all the cases emanated from one source, an attractive nymphomaniac then living in Scunthorpe. So, on the suggestion of the Station Medical Officer, Scunthorpe was placed out of bounds to all aircrew. 'If our surmise is correct,' wrote the MO in his monthly report, 'a remarkable fall in VD cases will be the result.' He was right. The following month no new cases were detected. However, in June cases started to increase again and by July, when we arrived there, they were growing at an alarming rate.

It was then discovered that the lady concerned, on hearing of the ban on young aircrew visiting Scunthorpe, had simply taken the bus to Gainsborough (four miles from Blyton), and had been able to pass on her affection, and affliction, to a whole new batch of men at the HCU.

During July and August the ban was still in force but was only half-heartedly applied and many crews, ours included, ran the gauntlet of service policemen. In fact, the senior officers were dismissing all charges against offenders who were caught. They had much greater problems with the chronic accident casualties from the clapped out Halifaxes crashing all over the place.

Germany's oil was again the target on 15 March when we set off at 5pm for the Deurag refinery at Misburg, on the outskirts of Hannover.

Our X-Ray 2 being in for overhaul we were flying U-Uncle 2. Up until now I had thought that all Lancs were good, some excellent, but Uncle 2 changed that. It turned out to be the worst Lancaster that I ever handled. For starters the automatic pilot was unserviceable and the engagement control was wired up so that it could not be used. On an eight hour plus sortie that was bad enough but I found that after carefully trimming the aircraft to fly 'hands off', she needed retrimming every time the gunners rotated their turrets. Normally a Lancaster yaws slightly right and left as the gunners rotate, searching their respective areas of the night sky, but the trim settings remain effective. The starboard inner engine was not performing as it should and try as I could, it would not synchronise with the other three, and occasionally surged giving off swathes of sparks from the exhaust.

Approaching the target on a heading of 353 degrees, we should have been at 19,000ft but Uncle 2 was labouring at just 16,000ft. Both Frank and Tubby reported Focke-Wulf and Messerschmitt 109s but the wild boars were attacking the bombers above us in the main stream and we carried out our attack unmolested. We learned later that four Lancasters had been shot down on our raid along with another 10 aircraft on a raid to Hagen, near Essen, the same night.

Landing back at Wickenby well after 1am, I stressed to Uncle's ground crew the unsatisfactory state of the starboard inner engine but their Flight Sergeant was not available. The starboard inner engine on a Lancaster is the most important one of the four. It is the one which was always started up first, as this engine ran the generators which charged the pneumatics and hydraulics which in turn operated the brakes, flaps, radiator shutters, undercarriage and all the other complex functions requiring hydraulic air pressure.

With only three ops to go I fully expected that I would never fly Uncle 2 again.

It was well after 2am by the time the debriefing and the meal was over. I was tired from my struggle with Uncle 2 and was thankful to get into bed.

Al Good joined me at the breakfast table with the news that we were on the ops list and that the aircraft were getting maximum fuel of 2,154 gallons. I said, 'Any whiff of the target?' Sometimes their leader informed the navigators if extra preparation was required although they were supposed to maintain strict secrecy. He whispered 'Nuremberg'.

Less than a year before Bomber Command had raided the city of Nuremberg in northern Bavaria. It turned into a major disaster with Bomber

Command suffering its heaviest loss of the war. Of the 779 bombers taking part 96 were missing; a total of 723 men dead, wounded or made prisoner in one night. As I mentioned earlier, in the whole duration of the Battle of Britain, 507 aircrew were killed whereas 545 bomber aircrew were killed within a few hours that one night.

On the board in the Flight Office I groaned when I saw that Uncle 2 was again our Lanc for tonight's raid. I approached the Flight Commander and asked for a change to the spare aircraft, stating that I thought it was near impossible for the starboard inner engine to have been made serviceable in the short time since we landed.

Sqr/Ldr Lane informed me that the spare Lanc was already committed to go on the operation and that the Squadron was struggling to meet its commitment. I was so concerned that I cycled out to Uncle's dispersal to check if anything was being done to the engine. I was relieved to see that the cowlings were off and the fitters were working on it, although I knew they could only change the spark plugs in the time available. Each engine on a Lancaster had 24 spark plugs.

Engine fitters were an elite band of mortals, ever resourceful and adaptable, whose skills, in common with their fellow airframe riggers, instrument technicians and others did not receive the recognition they deserved. But they could not perform miracles and Uncle 2's duff engine should have been replaced with a new one if there had been time before this important operation.

I would like to pay tribute at this point to the ground crews who themselves faced considerable risks in carrying out their vital tasks. For example part of the armourers' job was to select the requisite bombs listed for that night's raid and to arm each massive airborne weapon with the necessary fuses and detonators. Some fuses were set for explosion on impact, and others had built-in delays which would explode the bombs, sometimes hours after they had been dropped. This was a difficult task which required absolute concentration for obvious reasons. The long metal canisters filled with incendiary bombs also had to be made up and loaded into the aircraft. Wickenby was the scene of a serious accident during my time there in January 1945 when a bomb exploded prematurely, killing three armourers, just three of the 8,000 RAF ground crew killed in airfield accidents and through enemy action.

Here I can do no better than include the following poem written by one flight mechanic from 626 Squadron – Eric Sykes.

Three Cheers for the Man on the Ground

Wherever you walk, you will hear people talk,
Of the men who go up in the air.
Of the dare devil way, they go into the fray;
Facing death without turning a hair.

They'll raise a big cheer and buy lots of beer,
For a pilot who's home on leave;
But they dont give a jigger,
For a flight mech. or rigger,
With nothing but 'props' on his sleeve.

They just say 'Nice day' and then turn away,
With never a mention of praise.
And the poor bloody erk who does all the work;
Just orders his own beer,
And pays.

They've never been told, of the hours in the cold,
That he spends sealing Germany's fate.
How he works on a kite, till all hours of the night;
And then turns up next morning at eight.

He gets no rake off for working till take-off;
Or helping the aircrew prepare;

But whenever there's trouble, it's quick at the double;
The man on the ground must be there.

Each flying crew could tell it to you;
They know what this man's really worth.
They know he's a part of the RAF's heart,
Even though he stays close to the earth.

He doesn't want glory, but please tell his story;
Spread a little of his fame around.
He's one of the few, so give him his due;
Three cheers for the man on the ground.

* * * * *

At the main briefing for the Nuremberg raid we learned that we were to be part of a comparatively small force of Lancasters, all from 1 Group, numbering 230. It would be a clear night with no cloud and no moon. The bomb load was one 4,000lb blockbuster and 1,080 incendiaries (12 cans). Zero hour was at 9.30pm with the Pathfinders dropping the first cascade of red and green target indicators at 9.27pm. Take-off was to be around 5.30pm and the round trip would be over eight hours.

Looking at the route, marked with red ribbon on the large map behind the platform, gave me a feeling of apprehension. The long leg going through the gap in the flak defences between Karlsruhe and Mannheim, with only a slight alteration of course before overflying the city of Nuremberg, suggested to me that the German controllers would have an easy job guessing the target. Consequently we could expect the German night fighters to be on to us early.

The SIO pointed out the aiming point on the target map. It was in the southern part of the city where the main industries, the MAN (Machinen Augsburg Nurnburg) heavy engineering works and the two Siemens-Shuckertwerke electrical factories were situated. Also in that area were 46 other commercial plants plus 28 military and 16 Nazi Party establishments including a huge SS barracks near the Kongress Halle. A Master Bomber would control the bombing so that incoming bombers in the later waves would not be wasting their bombs on some factories and buildings which had already been flattened.

When the briefing ended, the senior officers returned to their offices while the crews trooped to the mess halls for what some wags called 'our Last Supper'.

Dusk was upon us as we made our way out to Uncle's dispersal. The Flt/Sgt informed me that as well as a set of new plugs, the starboard inner's exhaust stubs had been replaced. The old ones were badly burnt. He said there was nothing he could about the autopilot until the main overhaul.

The crackling roar of a Merlin starting up caused me to usher the crew aboard. When all four engines were running Don and I checked each one independently. The throttle was pushed to maximum take-off revs, and while at this speed the starboard magneto was switched off (making this mag dead). Immediately the rev-counter's pointer would fall registering the amount on the port mag, which was now the only one functioning on that engine. All engines showed a mag drop, sometimes very slight, but a maximum drop of 150rpm was allowed. Then the same procedure for checking the starboard mags was carried out. On the suspect engine the starboard mag dropped well over 200rpm but I decided to go.

By this time all the Squadron's aircraft had taxied out. We joined the queue of Lancasters slowly winding their way round the perimeter track to the take-off runway. Here we met No. 12 Squadron Lancasters coming from their dispersals.

It being a fine night there were many to wave us off. WAAFs with boyfriends on the raid, ground crews, clerks, anyone not otherwise occupied. Each bomber took its turn at the end of the runway and waited for a green from the controller's lamp. When our turn came there was only one other Lanc from 12 Squadron to take off after us. At 5.30pm precisely I pushed forward the throttle levers and Uncle 2 lumbered down the runway.

Due to the wind direction we were taking off on the short runway; only 1,400 yards. It seemed an eternity before Uncle reached its unstick speed of 105mph and we scraped over the boundary fence. Don gave a relieved 'thumb up' as we climbed away. Sitting as we were amid 12 tons of bombs and petrol, the failure of an engine could have resulted in a highly spectacular end to our tour.

Maintaining full power up to 2,000ft, Don and I knew there was little improvement in the SI engine. It would not synchronise and occasionally surged. I knew then that I was in for another hard night. Throttling back to standard climbing power, we continued to circle. The absence of enemy intruders allowed us to use our navigation lights, and the clear conditions made it comparatively safe from collisions. Eventually at 8,000ft Al gave me a course for Reading.

Switching on the superchargers at 12,000ft, I could see nearby bombers switching off their navigation lights and did likewise. Just about then I spotted two Lancasters below with nav lights on returning to their bases. Obviously they had experienced some technical trouble. There were some unavoidable cases where to proceed was impossible. However, there was also the in-between position where the defect was such as to allow the aircraft to carry on if in the hands of a 'press on' crew but where equally a less resolute one could return with a reasonable excuse. Early returns failed to count as an operation towards the tour unless bombs had been dropped on some enemy target, but many crews were quite happy to forego this in exchange for the release from a particularly difficult raid. I say crews but the decision is always the pilot's. I found on our return that one of our Squadron aircraft did return early, but in that case Flying Officer Fisk had two badly functioning engines.

Al came on the intercom informing me that we were about to cross the Channel at Hastings. I waited until we were well over the water before giving the gunners permission to test their guns. Frank and Tubby fired bursts as short as possible; they were unwilling to waste a single round of ammunition more than was necessary. Al was working hard to get the vital accurate fixes that would tell him how the actual winds compared with those forecast. His Gee box was giving a succession of good positions but the Germans would soon jam this aid. I was pleased with the way Al had settled in with the crew. He had won our respect; he had always been cool but his navigation skills had improved greatly. Greg had wound out his trailing aerial and had only to listen in to the Group broadcasts every half-hour. Stan had been forward to fuse the bombs and check his panel and was now working the H2S screen, helping Al. Don was continually checking our fuel consumption and monitoring the 20 or so gauges. He was continually adjusting the amount of fuel in the six tanks so that if a tank was holed the loss was limited. At night, forward of the navigator's blackout curtain, there wasn't much light about, only the luminosity of the instruments, so Don used a shaded torch to record in his log sheet. Most pilots preferred their engineer's eyes to be looking out of the cockpit, scanning for enemy fighters.

Approaching our turning point on the river Meuse, five miles south of Verdun, I was still struggling with Uncle to reach our bombing height of 18,000ft. I eventually made it to 17,000ft only to find on setting cruising controls that Uncle sank to 16,000ft. To conserve our fuel we stayed there. Most pilots tried to gain as much height as possible and a good Lancaster with a full load could usually make it above 22,000ft. Each pilot at briefing was given a specific altitude to fly and if everyone adhered to that the bomber stream would be uniform and compact. But many pilots crept up to their maximum height, which was undoubtedly safer, but which left those who stuck to their lower allocated heights more isolated.

We were now on a course of 090 degrees true and heading for the Karlsruhe – Mannheim gap. I could sense the increased alertness and tension in the crew. A long ribbon of white fire splayed out on the ground, probably another Lancaster that could not get height jettisoning his incendiaries. To me, an Aberdonian, that action was unthinkable – what a waste.

Visibility was good and I could see other Lancasters above us blotting out the stars. Frank reported a Ju 88 crossing starboard to port 2,000ft above. A short time later a Lancaster high on our port burst into flames, and as he fell it could not have been more than 10 seconds before he exploded with a huge orange flash.

I was puzzled as there was no flak and I had not seen any tracers. Even if the gunners had not seen the German fighter I should have seen his tracer shells as I was looking at that part of the sky when the Lancaster was hit. It must have been only four minutes or so before another bomber trailed fire then blew up. My worst fears in the briefing room were happening. Nuremberg was still 270 miles away and the German fighters were among us. If confirmation was needed that the German controllers knew our route, a line of fighter flares now appeared ahead. This was soon followed by another, then another until it seemed that we were on a well-lit main road. I had often seen German fighter flares before but not so numerous as this night and not so near. These pale red parachute flares seemed to burn a long time.

I decided that the stream was too dangerous and eased out a few miles to starboard. I told Stan to stop Windowing. I also had Greg in the astrodome and Don searching above while Tubby and Frank searched below the aircraft while I carried out continuous weaving. Two more Lancs were shot down as we turned at our last place called Heilbron on our run up to Nuremberg. The bomber stream's 30-degree change of course was again marked with fresh fighter flares.

On the last hundred miles to Nuremberg five more Lancs went down. Three blew up within seconds and I watched two on fire go all the way before blowing up on the ground. At least the crews on them had a chance to escape by parachute.

This was my 35th operation and I had never seen so many bombers shot down before reaching the target. I was 22 years old and was wondering if I would see 23.

One more Lancaster streaming fire blew up not far ahead and slightly port. He was so close that I thought we would suffer serious damage flying through his debris but only felt a few rattles on our fuselage.

The target appeared 20 miles ahead and amid the searchlights and flak, red and green target indicators cascaded at exactly 21:27 hours. The Master Bomber came on the air ordering incoming bombers to aim at the centre of the tight bunch of red and green markers. Stan called, 'Left left, left left, left left, steady,...steady...bombs away.' At that most welcome call I thrust the throttles fully forward and stuffed the nose down to build up speed. When I was sure the photograph was taken, I pulled hard round on to a southerly course, then turned west for home.

Looking back at Nuremberg, I could see the southern part of the city well ablaze with huge clouds of black smoke rising above 3,000ft. Wild Boar fighters were now attacking the bombers leaving the target and red and yellow tracer bullets arced against the starlit sky. Frank and Tubby both reported combats taking place well above us. It was maybe just as well that Uncle 2 was unable to reach our designated altitude of 18,000ft or we would have been more involved in all the action.

Fresh lines of fighter flares were appearing ahead marking the bombers' route out. I still had the throttles full open and showers of sparks were now flying from the starboard inner engine's exhaust stubs. The temperature on its gauge was dangerously high and Don said, 'Jock you had better throttle back a bit or the starboard inner will blow up'. I said, 'Bugger the engine, if it packs in we'll feather it, the other three are good'. I knew that Don was more concerned with the fuel consumption than the engine so once we were well on our way I let him reduce revs on all four.

Passing well to the north of Stuttgart we eventually came to the French town of Nancy where we turned on to a course of 330 degrees. My mouth was as dry as a bone. I tapped Don on the shoulder and signalled that I could do with a cup of coffee. The poor gunners would have to wait until we were much nearer home before getting theirs.

Crossing the English coast, the SI engine was at last stopped and feathered. We landed at Wickenby on three engines at 1.45am, having been in the air for a total of eight and a quarter hours. We were collected from the aircraft and taken back to the crew rooms. After disposing of parachutes, flying suits and equipment we went straight in to debriefing. I stressed to the Intelligence Officer that of the 10 bombers I had witnessed being shot down, I had not seen any tracers either from the bomber or the fighter. Obviously the bombers were being hit from underneath without the gunners detecting the fighters. The IO wrote down my statement without comment. He looked tired, poor chap, waiting all that time for us to return! I have heard since that the *Schrage Musik* guns did in fact use faint blue tracer shells.

Later that day we learned that seven Lancasters failed to return to Wickenby from Nuremberg. Six were from 12 Squadron although one had landed in France and one was lost from 626 Squadron, piloted by F/Lt L.J. Cox. (F/L Cox and two of his crew, F/O S. Quinn and Sgt R. Noessen, survived the crash although injured and were hospitalised in captivity for five weeks until liberation.) In all, however, 24 Lancasters, all from 1 Group, were lost which was 10.4 per cent of the 1 Group aircraft involved. This was to be the last great success the German Luftwaffe would enjoy.

CHAPTER 18
TOUR'S END

Because of the mauling 1 Group had suffered we were stood down for two days after Nuremberg. Then, on 19 March, we were briefed to raid Hanau, an important junction in the German railway system, about 10 miles east of Frankfurt. Thankfully Uncle 2 had been taken out for overhaul and repairs and we flew in O-Oboe 2. What a pleasure it was to fly a good Lancaster again with a serviceable 'George' to share the piloting. We also had a new navigator, F/O Foy, a New Zealander. His Captain, F/O Warner, had been our 'second dickey' on the Stuttgart op.

F/O Al Good had been transferred to a new Canadian crew whose navigator had been wounded on the Nuremberg raid.

Taking off at 30 minutes after midnight we were over the target at 4.30am. Stan obeyed the Master Bomber's instruction to give a one-second overshoot on the green TIs. Flak was slight but there was some fighter activity and Frank reported a Lancaster going down in flames as we sped away from the target. We landed back at Wickenby at 8am and later heard that the raid was highly successful.

Now we only had one more operation to complete our extended tour. It was Wednesday 21 March 1945. At the late afternoon briefing, we learned that 12

Lancasters from 626 Squadron were to be part of a total force of 130, which were to bomb the Bruchstrasse Benzol Plant at Bochum, about eight miles east of Essen in the Ruhr. Not exactly an easy one for our last trip. However, we had Oboe 2 again and I was happy for that. Our bomb load was a 'cookie', 12 500lb and four 250lb HE bombs.

Our navigator for the night was Warrant Officer Potter, whose regular Skipper was F/O Tierney, a Canadian. Bill Potter was also a Canadian and had missed a few ops with his crew because of illness. He was an affable chap and an able navigator.

The crew bus took us out to Oboe's dispersal half an hour after midnight. There were no high spirits with the crew as we were all acutely aware that an inordinately high number of crews got the chop on their very last operation.

Taking off at 46 minutes past midnight, we were on the bombing run at 18,000ft heading 070 degrees true. The night was clear and there were over 30 searchlights operating. Stan was giving me directions when a huge red flash followed by flames and black smoke showed that someone had hit the jackpot. Stan gave 'bombs away' and seconds later I turned sharply to port to escape northwestward.

All the way home I had the throttles full open and maximum revs. When we crossed the English coast Greg said, 'Can I fire off all my Very cartridges, Jock?' I said, 'OK but not our distress colours.' Greg then proceeded to shoot off the Very pistol. Multi-coloured flares banged out of Oboe and arced backwards; it was like Guy Fawkes Night.

Arriving back in the circuit long before any other Lancaster, I called up, 'Oboe 2, permission to land'. The soft voice of the WAAF R/T operator was music to our ears – 'Congratulations Flying Officer Yule and crew, call funnels.'

Taxiing into dispersal at 6.45am, the crew bus was waiting. Piling our gear in I asked the driver to take us to Roger 2 and X-Ray 2's dispersals where I told the ground crews – 'Tonight, we all go out and get pissed. It's on us, we will be at the Saracen's Head in Lincoln at opening time.'

I bought the first round, Stan got the second, Don got in the third and then I lost count. We toasted the ground crew every round. When we were well on

I said that we probably wouldn't get in another tour over Europe, but would they be willing to be in my crew again on a tour over Japan? It was gratifying to hear 'Sure Jock, we would go anywhere with you', even though they were all pie-eyed by this time.

During our leave the Allies bridged the Rhine and the last phase of the land war had started. The Squadron was grounded for much of the time but 626 was unfortunate in the raids that were carried out, three complete crews being killed. Those of F/Lt Eames and F/O Driver, both experienced and well on their tours, and F/O Reid, a Canadian who had just arrived on the Squadron with his crew less than four weeks before. For a family to lose a son so near to victory is very sad.

Back at Wickenby, after a long leave, I looked at the notice board for news of our postings and found it briefly stated:

F/O R.C.Yule 187294 Pilot to 1660 H.C.U.

F/S F.O.Fathers 1037404 A/G to A.C.A.C.

F/S A. Clayton 2221649 A/G to A.C.A.C.

F/S G. Leader 1594213 F/E to A.C.A.C.

Also, P/O E.S. Moore A/B A417662 to A.C.A.C. Stan had at last got his well-deserved commission. There was no word of Greg. The Adjutant then contacted me with the news that I had to get my gear together and was to be flown in the spare Lancaster to Swinderby, near Nottingham. I had barely time to get my clearance chit signed by all the departments before being bundled into a Lancaster with my kitbag and bicycle and flown to Swinderby. I had no time to say goodbye to the crew.

That night, 12 April 1945, feeling lonely and miserable, I was sitting in a pub in Newark with a pint of beer. I was thinking of the crew and realised that we came together exactly one year ago today. The memories flooded back – the good times, the dangers and the laughs. Now it was all over and I was wondering whether we would ever see each other again.

For the remainder of April I was engaged as a screen pilot instructing sprog crews on Lancasters. I had confirmation around this time that notice of my award of the DFC (Distinguished Flying Cross) had appeared in the *London Gazette.* On 30 April, my 23rd birthday, Hitler committed suicide in Berlin after handing over the leadership of Germany to Admiral Doenitz.

During May and June I was at No. 3 Flying Instructors School at Lulsgate Bottom, near Bristol. We flew Air Speed Oxfords on the course. I got my Flying Instructor's Certificate but my heart was not on this type of flying job. It was here that news came through that Germany had surrendered and the war in Europe was over.

* * * * *

Returning to Swinderby after leave in Aberdeen, I was engaged in flying Lancasters with parties of ground staff to show them the devastation of Germany's cities. From less than 1,000ft it was an incredible sight to see acres, almost square miles in fact, of roads lined with ruined buildings. The sun shone through rows of glassless holes in the walls where windows used to be. Not a single roof remained in this vast honeycomb of brick walls.

Flying over Duisburg, Essen, Dortmund, Cologne and Dusseldorf I now felt remorse for all the innocent people who suffered. Not so long ago when I was up there high above, I was too concerned for my own skin to have any sympathy for those having to endure the horrors on the ground.

There are those who say that the German people deserved retribution but who can equate Hitler, Himmler and the monsters of the Nazi extermination camps with ordinary soldiers, airmen, workers and their families?

One person asked me long after the war, how could I drop bombs knowing that women and children would be killed? I replied until after Dresden, I never thought I was. If it was an industrial city, I thought that if the women and children were not already evacuated, there would be deep, safe bomb shelters.

All the targets after Dresden I considered to be legitimate industrial, military and quasi-military objectives. I would have felt revulsion at the thought of destroying life where there was no immediate military target.

Dresden, however, remains on my conscience. It was the only target where there was no opposition whatsoever. It still makes me squirm if images of the devastation we wreaked appear on television or in newsprint.

For years I blamed Butch Harris for choosing the target, and that he should have known it was more or less an 'open city'. I now know that Bomber Command was specifically requested by the Air Ministry under Sir Charles Portal, with Winston Churchill's encouragement, to carry out heavy raids on Dresden, Chemnitz and Leipzig which were all cities just behind the German lines on the Eastern Front. On 4 February, at the Yalta Conference, the Russians had asked for attacks of this kind to take place, but this only came after the relevant directive had been issued by the Air Ministry to Bomber Command. The Americans were also asked to help and agreed to do so. The campaign should have begun with an American raid on Dresden on 13 February but bad weather prevented this and it thus fell to Bomber Command to carry out the first raid.

Even so, how can you blame men like Churchill or Harris, with the awesome responsibilities on their shoulders? It is sufficient, I think, to recognise that their priorities were to eliminate German resistance and bring the war to as rapid a conclusion as possible thus minimising further Allied losses.

At the end of the war, Bomber Command received the courtesies of victory but, beneath a layer of perfunctory goodwill, it was soon apparent that in the safety of peace the bombers' part in the war was one that many politicians and civilians would prefer to forget. Indeed Churchill tried to distance himself from the Dresden raid afterwards. The laurels and the romantic adulation were reserved for Fighter Command, the defenders.

Beyond those who died flying for Bomber Command, their relatives and surviving aircrews often felt and today still feel deeply betrayed by criticism of the strategic offensive. It is wrong that this should have been so. We aircrew of Bomber Command went out to do what we were told had to be done for Britain and Allied victory, and subsequent judgements on the bomber offensive can do nothing to mar the honour of such an epitaph.

Bomber County

The skies are empty now that darkness falls,
The bare deserted runways scarred with weeds,
Across the lonely fen a night bird calls,
The wind sighs softly in the whispering reeds.

A fitful moon rides through the cloudy blue,
A bomber's moon, remembered now no more,
Where once the very air vibrated to,
The mighty Merlin engine's roar.

Dispersal huts stand crumbling and forlorn,
Their broken windows open to the rain,
The taxi track is fringed with waving corn,
The echoing hangars used for storing grain.

Upon the cracking tarmac wander sheep,
A derelict crew room door creaks in the breeze,
The silent world around is lost in sleep,
And stars are twinkling far above the trees.

Those very stars which were a friendly aid,
To those who flew upon the wings of night,
The crews who never grudged the price they paid,
To keep aglow the flame of freedom's right.

There is no flarepath now to show the way,
And guide the homing bombers to the ground,
The old control tower stands in gaunt decay,
In silence and in darkness wrapt around.

Remember those who flew, across the years,
Those bright young lives they gave so long ago,
No looking back with bitterness or tears,
But thankfulness – for they would wish it so.
By Audrey Grealy

CHAPTER 19

POST-WAR YEARS

After my stint flying ground staff over the devastated German cities, Winnie and I were married in Aberdeen in October 1945. I then spent the next six months stationed in Yorkshire, latterly at Linton-on-Ouse, training on the new Halifax 7s to qualify as a transport pilot and thus gain my transport command licence. During this period I came under increasing pressure to sign on a permanent commission. However, I resisted this because I knew that it would mean being posted to Palestine for two years without any prospect of taking my wife with me. Accordingly, I effectively stalled for time in the hope that I might be offered a different posting but, in August 1946, when at 16 Ferry Unit, St Mawgan, Cornwall, I was unconditionally released from the RAF having still declined to sign on. That was a decision I came to regret as my prospects of rapid advancement would undoubtedly have been excellent had I agreed to stay on.

In any event it was back to 'civvy street' for me and I returned to A. Hall & Co. in order to complete my unfinished apprenticeship as a marine engineer. I achieved this in August 1947 and then stayed on there as a journeyman fitter until November 1948.

In the meantime, in January 1947, I had joined 612 squadron of the Auxiliary Air Force, based at Dyce, Aberdeen. I accepted a post as Flight Sergeant because there were no vacancies for commissioned officers at that time and I badly wanted the opportunity to fly again. However, before long I was reinstated to Flying Officer and then promoted to Flight Lieutenant. Before that happened though my DFC on a sergeant's uniform always attracted considerable attention.

612 Squadron had been revived as from 1 November 1946 and its first establishment of aircraft comprised six Spitfire Mark XIVs, plus two Harvard Trainers for dual or solo work. S/Ldr Ramsay Russell, a wartime Coastal Command Squadron commander was appointed Auxiliary commanding Officer and regular officers providing the necessary back-up initially included F/Lt Len Cherry as Adjutant and F/Lt Jock Dalgleish as Training Officer. The reformed Squadron was looking for youngish, experienced single-engined pilots but there weren't so many of them around Aberdeen. However, the first six NCOs who came in as Sergeant Pilots were myself, Johnny Milne, Jim Healy, Alan Mitchell, Hector Melvin and Sandy Gordon. We became firm friends along with others who came into the fold afterwards and I remained with 612 until its disbandment in March 1957.

We shared some wonderful times in those 10 years and ever a highlight were the summer camps which were held in July each year. The first such camp, in 1947, was at RAF Woodvale, near Southport, but because of poor weather and facilities this one was not nearly as memorable as some of those which followed.

In May 1948, the Spitfire XIVs were suddenly withdrawn from Squadron service for sale to India who were looking for fighter aircraft with an altitude capability. 612 received eight almost brand new Spitfire XVIs as replacements and these, with their Merlin engines, were more powerful and better suited to general flying. Jim Healy and I were taken down to Llandow in North Wales to collect two of the new aircraft and take them back to Dyce. This we duly achieved but only after some alarming moments in the air before we both managed to suss out that the throttle system was significantly different to that on the Mark XIV.

Summer camp in July 1948 was held at RAF Menston near Ramsgate in Kent. By then, a number of other pilots had come in including Bill Thom, Nigel McLean, Bill Innes, Roddy McKay, Pat Pattullo, Roddy Robertson and Doug Robertson. Doug had recently married Sheila who was one of my wife's best friends and he was already a good pal of mine. He had flown a couple of operations with Bomber Command just before the end of the war and I was instrumental in getting him into 612.

While at Ramsgate, Jock Dalgleish and I paid a visit to Dinard in Brittany to take part in an air display. My Spitfire developed a mechanical fault so we had to send for the mechanics who wouldn't be able to arrive in France until the following day. Accordingly Jock and I spent the night over there as guests of the French officer in charge of the airfield. Before hitting the bars in Rennes he plied us with several glasses of cognac at his house and I have no recollection whatsoever of the latter stages of that evening. The next day, the mechanic, Alex Nicol arrived from Kent to effect the repair and, feeling extremely rough, I executed what must have been the worst slow roll I ever did after taking off.

Squadron Leader Joe Child, who had been chosen as Regular Commanding Officer to succeed Ramsay Russell who was leaving the following month, was at the Menston camp. He was well-liked by all and it was a sad loss when his Spitfire went into the ground in September after our formation got into the Cu-nim cloud over Northumberland which I described in chapter 6.

Some other potential pilots were enrolled in the first half of 1949, including Ian Scorgie and Trevor Smith, who was a teacher at Aberdeen Grammar School when I worked there as a janitor for a spell (more of that later). That summer the Squadron went to Thorney Island with its full complement of eight Spitfires and two Harvards. My wife was able to come with me and it was an excellent camp with good location, weather and accommodation. Not long after returning to Dyce we received the news that the Auxiliary Squadrons were being transferred from Reserve Command to Fighter Command and 612 Squadron now came under direct control of 13 Group of the Command. Around this time I reached the finals of the auxiliary inter-squadron races held at Elmdon, Birmingham. I only finished fifth – about a minute behind the winner – but I can't resist pointing out that the Spitfire XV that I was flying was one of the oldest aircraft in the race!

An active training programme continued throughout the winter and early in 1950 one benefit of the change of strategic group command was apparent when the Press carried the announcement that the Scottish Auxiliary Squadrons would spend their summer camp on the island of Sylt, just off the coast of north-west Germany close to the border with Denmark.

We flew the aircraft to Sylt by way of Linton-on-Ouse, Manston, Eindhoven and Wunstorf, the remainder of the personnel being air-lifted straight from Leuchars. By early evening the whole Squadron was settled in comfortable accommodation in the former Luftwaffe base now being used as a gunnery training airfield by the RAF. It had everything needed for an ideal camp – good flying and firing facilities, an excellent location on a German holiday resort packed with tourists, a holiday town in nearby Westerland with a casino, bars and every facility for a good time, gorgeous beaches and good swimming in the North Sea. At certain beaches named 'Abyssinia', it turned out that nudist bathing was the order of the day. The first sight a party of us had of this though was rather off-putting when we came in view of this gross middle-aged woman wearing only a bathing cap who was scampering into the sea leading a squadron of young children behind her. Compensation was soon to follow, however, when we arrived at this café at the top of the dunes and saw a quite stunning blonde reclining on a basket chair wearing nothing but a large hat. After seating ourselves no one was prepared to move before she did. It's funny how certain things stay in your mind but the memory of the imprint of the basket chair on her posterior when she did eventually get up is certainly one of those for me.

Those who participated in the camp at Sylt were generally agreed that it was the outstanding camp in our Auxiliary experience. A reporter, George Hutcheon, and a photographer, Herbert Imlah, from the *Aberdeen Press and Journal* accompanied the Squadron, so the newspaper published daily details and pictures of the activities – although not quite all of them mercifully! By the end of the first week their expense accounts were all used up and they requested a top-up from their editor. Instead they were peremptorily summoned home but as they would have to wait for the return Hastings flight to Leuchars they spent the second week effectively as guests of the Squadron who paid for all their drinks and so on. They were both great lads though and George was unfailingly supportive of the Squadron in his reporting over the years. A couple of years after Sylt he was responsible for a cartoon appearing in the P&J which depicted someone driving a motorcycle with L plates on before taking to the skies behind the controls of a jet aircraft. Everyone knew that this was based on me – I didn't pass my driving test until late 1953 by which time I had been flying Vampire and Meteor jets for over two years.

* * * * *

By late 1950, 612 Squadron was earmarked for conversion jet training at RAF Leuchars following a decision that a jet capable runway was to be built at Dyce. Then, in January 1951, the escalation of the war in Korea and other disturbances in the Middle East and elsewhere led to the Prime Minister making an announcement in the House of Commons of the proposed short term mobilisation of the Auxiliary Squadrons. The 612 Squadron members eventually checked into Leuchars to start the call-up on Sunday 16 July 1951. That same evening, myself, Roddy Robertson and Trevor Smith were detailed to be flown, first thing the next morning, to the De Havilland factory at Hawarden, Cheshire, to pick up three new Vampires awaiting collection.

Now, a Meteor 7 and a Vampire 5 had been sited at RAF Leuchars for the use of 612 personnel since the beginning of June. However, although most of the pilots including myself had managed at least one trip there for familiarisation flights in both aircraft, we had not received the promised pilot's notes and the ground crews invariably had the engines already running when we approached an aircraft to fly it.

So, on arrival at Hawarden, the three of us picked up our bundles of documents and parachutes and trooped out to the aircraft where we got ourselves strapped in. After briefly twiddling with the controls, it suddenly dawned on me to my consternation that I had never started one of these kites before and on looking across I could tell that Roddy was in the same boat. I couldn't see Trevor from where I was but it turned out that he was in the same predicament.

Now more than a little red-faced, I beckoned one of the two ground crew who were standing by their trolley to come up on to the wing beside the cockpit. I then asked him if he could tell me how to start the aircraft. He thought I was taking the mickey at first but when he realised I was serious he shouted down to his mate, 'You're never going to believe this but he doesn't even know how to start the bloody thing!'

Eventually, and not without some hesitation, they accepted our assurances that if they just showed us how to start up we were perfectly capable of flying the aircraft. The taxi out and take-off were then watched with great interest by quite a crowd who had streamed out of the huts as we moved out. Everything went smoothly until we arrived at the dispersal back at Leuchars. We then had to ask how to switch off the aircraft and you may be sure that the solitary available copy of the pilot's notes got close study during the next few days. None of us were going to get caught out again.

I can laugh when I look back on that episode. However, tragedy was to strike during our time at Leuchars when firstly, Jim Thompson crashed in a Vampire due to an oxygen problem and then Doug Robertson and Roddy McKay were killed on a dual flight in a Meteor 7 which went into the ground when they were practising single engine flying. Doug was my best pal and about four years previously we were seriously planning to emigrate to Canada with our wives until an unforeseen and massive hike in the fares put paid to this.

The call-up lasted only three months and ended on 16 October 1951. For me that meant going back to work as a janitor at Walker Road School in Torry, Aberdeen, while still, of course, continuing to fly at weekends and at summer camps. Our daughter Lesley had been born on 7 July 1947 and within three months it was confirmed that she was suffering from a severe form of mental handicap. Until that point my plans had been to go to sea as a marine engineer. However, the priority then became to try and secure a reasonably well paid job with a free house if possible and in November 1948 I left A. Hall & Co. to take up a post at Torry Academy before transferring to Walker Road.

* * * * *

The new 2,000yd runway at Dyce Airfield was completed between midsummer 1951 and late autumn 1952 and ultimately did much to ensure the development of the airfield into what is now Aberdeen Airport. It remained the basis of the new 17/35 runway when the airport was reconstructed and developed into a fully equipped modern airport during the 1970s. Accordingly, at the end of the call-up the Squadron aircraft were flown to RAF Edzell and for the next year this was to be the home of 612. It was located some 34 miles South of Aberdeen in a pleasant part of Kincardineshire and because personal transport in those days was still relatively rare, most of the auxiliaries had to be bused there from Aberdeen at weekends. I was fortunate to often get a lift from Peter Gray, who had recently joined us, and we became good friends. It was when the Squadron was based at Edzell that my son Royan junior was born on 30 December so Hogmanay the next night was an extra special celebration for me.

In the spring of 1952 we received intimation that 612 was to be rewarded for the call-up by a camp in Malta. Tropical kitting started in June and we were impressed when we witnessed the the delivery of the huge underwing overload tanks for the Vampires. None of us had flown with these long range tanks on before.

I was one of the pilots who flew the 10 Vampires out to Takali in Malta by way of North Weald in Essex and Istres in Southern France. The four Hastings which followed carried a total of 160 airmen and the rest of the officers. On arrival in Malta it was blistering hot and the ground crew of the regular resident squadron welcomed us with a pint of cold beer before we had even got out of the aircraft. When I think of it now it reminds me of the final scene in the film, *Ice Cold in Alex* when Sir John Mills stares at his glass for a few moments before downing it in one.

The camp at Takali was a fantastic experience for all concerned when you bear in mind that overseas holidays were an unknown indulgence for the great majority in those days. All of the services who formed the island garrison, RAF, Navy and HLI (Highland Light Infantry) went out of their way to provide hospitality. Our Accountant Officer, Andy Cooper, was a pal of Ronnie Tulloch, an Aberdonian who was manager of the local Anchor Brewery, so we were kept well supplied with the amber nectar.

I had a fair amount of scope to do more or less as I pleased once airborne and on one memorable occasion I decided to fly my Vampire up to Sicily. There was some cloud cover when I got there but I still managed to fly over Mount Etna and look down on the crater before swooping down the other side. I suspect that we had a lot more latitude to do things like that on the spur of the moment than would be the case these days!

After a great two weeks in Malta we flew back to Edzell by way of El Ouina in Tunisia, Istres and an overnight stay at Tangmere in Sussex before completing the trip.

The long awaited runway at Dyce was finally completed in October so on 2 November we refuelled at Edzell for the last time and flew back to our home base.

Over the next few months our CO, S/Ldr Guy Cory was replaced by an Auxiliary, Nigel McLean, his senior flight commander who managed a Civil Engineering company in Aberdeen. The regular officers attached to the Squadron, F/Lt N. Townsend, Adjutant, and F/Lt Sid Walker, Training Officer also completed their tours with 612 and were replaced by F/Lt Tim De Salis and F/Lt Tony Madden respectively.

The coming Coronation on 2 June then required flying practice for a formation over Aberdeen and also more drill than usual because the Squadron was to participate in a big military parade in Aberdeen on the morning of Coronation day.

Summer camp in 1953 was at Thorney Island where we had been four years before. Socially it was a great success but problems with unserviceability and lack of spares blighted the business side of things. Then almost as soon as we got back to Dyce it was time to practice for the Battle of Britain air display which was to take place in September and was to become a regular feature of the Dyce calendar, attracting 15–20,000 spectators to aerial and static displays. It was at this first such event that Jim Healy engineered a memorable spoof on the local press which was reported in banner headlines: 'SOUND BARRIER BROKEN OVER DYCE IN AIR DISPLAY'.

I knew in advance, of course, that Jim planned to initiate a power dive over the airfield, and at an appropriate moment field regiment auxiliaries fired off two blanks from a hidden Bofors gun in quick succession just before Jim zoomed away again. It sounded very convincing and only the more knowledgeable (or those in the know) were not taken in.

The site chosen for the 1954 camp was the major airfield at RAF Bruggen in Germany. Although eagerly anticipated this turned out to be a major disappointment owing to the consistently bad weather. This impacted on the social side as well because persistent fog and mist in the mornings meant that flying was transferred to the afternoon and early evening. This did not go down too well with us auxiliaries who had given up our holidays to attend camp and didn't appreciate cancellations of off-duty time. However, we couldn't complain too vociferously because the flying practice was after all the main object of the whole exercise.

The following spring, we took part in the major Exercise 'Skyhigh', which simulated an invasion of the UK by the forces of a foreign power (no prizes for guessing who was envisaged in this context). As was invariably the case our performance in executing low and medium level interceptions received good reports. However, the rate of climb nullified any success for the aircraft we had (still Vampires and a couple of Meteor 7s) against high altitude (above 45,000ft) intruders such as the Canberras deployed in this exercise. Accordingly, by this time speculation had become rife regarding the future role of the Royal Auxiliary Air force and, should it have a role, the choice of aircraft to enable it to be carried out effectively.

A happy and successful camp was held in July at RAF Coltishall in Norfolk. It was then back to prepare for the autumn exercise, 'Beware' which consisted of RAF bombers simulating high-level attacks against major east coast towns, all interceptions being carried out by aircraft situated on the east side of the country including, of course, Dyce. Again, however, while the more modern Hunters from RAF Leuchars were reporting great success, we could only report the Canberras penetrating well above our maximum altitude. It was clear that if this was the future role envisaged for the Auxiliaries then we would have to be re-equipped or else disbanded.

For the last two years of its existence the Squadron enjoyed good press publicity in the form of a a regular feature, 'Airstrip' in the local *Evening Express* of which George Hutcheon, who had accompanied us to camp at Sylt in 1950, was now an editor. I featured in a (slightly cringeworthy!) article under the heading – 'Flying Janitor is the Schoolboys' Hero' – which had a photograph of me entering the cockpit of my Vampire jet. By then I was employed as a janitor at Ruthrieston Junior Secondary School on Holburn Street, Aberdeen.

As the reader will no doubt have gleaned by now, summer camp was invariably the highlight of an auxiliary squadron's year and always eagerly looked forward to. What turned out to be our last one was held at RAF Thornaby, in North Yorkshire, in July 1956. We flew all of our aircraft, 10 Vampires and two Meteors, down there and the weather was superb for the first week at least. Important visitors included Air Commodore Finlay Crerar, an ADC to the Queen and AVM John Cheshire of 13 Group.

Socially it was a tremendous camp and I believe that our farewell party on the last Friday was one of the biggest and most successful events in the history of Thornaby. Although we didn't yet know it, this was to be the last camp most of us would ever attend.

Soon, rumours of 'disbandment' were very much in the foreground and then, early in January 1957, the news was delivered in the House of Commons that all auxiliary flying and field regiment squadrons would be disbanded almost immediately with the terminal date set at 10 March 1957.

The farewell social functions were duly held including the 'Disbandment Ball' at the beginning of March. These were enjoyable and successful despite the occasional 'wake' atmosphere. The last day for the Squadron to assemble was set for 17 February when, led by the Gordon Highlanders Pipe Band, we paraded for the last time down Union Street, Aberdeen, past the Music Hall where the Lord Provost, George Stephen, took the salute, then on to the West Church of St Nicholas for a disbandment service. In the afternoon the Squadron assembled at Dyce for a farewell group photograph and then it was all over, barring our annual get togethers which were held latterly at the Dee Motel, Aberdeen.

Chapter 20

A VOICE FROM THE PAST

The year was 1981. The war, Lancasters and Wickenby were farthest from my mind when I answered the telephone in my home in Dundee, one day in late August. 'This is a voice from the past. Does the name Arthur mean anything to you?' I said, 'No but "Tubby Clayton" does – while you were talking I recognised your voice'. Tubby then went on to inform me that he had phoned every Yule in the Aberdeen telephone directory before finally getting my son's number who informed him of my address.

Tubby was now living in Nettleton, a small village near Caistor only 10 miles north of Wickenby. He was employed as a Cold Storage Supervisor with a famous Lincoln chicken-processing firm.

The purpose of his call was that he had just heard there was to be a dedication service to a memorial now standing at Wickenby on Sunday 6 September 1981. The memorial stone had been raised by ex-12 and 626 Squadron members to the 1,127 men who gave their lives on air operations from Wickenby. He wondered if I could attend and if I knew of any of the other crew members' addresses. I only knew Stan's address in Australia but arranged to meet Tubby in Caistor on the Saturday before the dedication.

Tubby had booked me into an old world hotel in Caistor called the 'Floral' where every window had a well-stocked flower box. The building was very old and had creaky stairs lined with ornaments, copperware, etc. Later that night, after a great pub crawl with Tubby, I was forced to water the flowers outside my bedroom window. The toilet was on the next floor upstairs and after two or three journeys to the loo, the ornaments clanked and clinked, the banisters and stair treads squeaked horribly and to top it all, the ancient cistern gushed like the Niagara Falls. Approaching 3am I was again in torment and was actually regretting all the pints of beer I had drunk. I just could not face causing any more din so decided to be the good watering can fairy to the plants on the sill.

On Sunday morning Tubby took me on a tour of the Wickenby airfield, pointing out the various sites including the space where the hut used to be when we were billeted with the army lads, the areas where the Squadron offices and briefing room used to be and Roger 2 and X-Ray 2s' dispersals.

Of all the places that a man can return to, an old battlefield or an old airfield must be the place most laden with meaning. For aircrew the battlefield was a shifting sky, a lonely sky. We therefore often have to be content with a patch of rugged ground that has no special symbol on a map.

The memories flooded back as Tubby and I walked about the silent airfield, especially the heavy feeling in the stomach before climbing aboard a Lancaster bound for a heavily defended German target. The great feeling when we landed, even though we might have to go back again the same night. The happy times when we were all together in the same hut and sharing the same Sergeant's mess before I got commissioned. Then Tubby's voice broke into my reverie, 'Thirty-seven years ago almost to the day Jock – let's go to the White Hart for a pint'.

A good number of people had gathered at the White Hart in the small hamlet of Lissington, just a couple of miles north of Wickenby. The sun was shining and the landlord had erected a large marquee to cater for the large crowd expected.

A face I instantly remembered was our bombing leader Tom Wardle. One memorable night during the winter of 1944, the gales off the North Sea had brought in some really murky weather and ops were off for a few days. We had a sing song round the piano with all the disreputable songs of the time – *The*

Old Monk, Frigging in the Rigging, Twas on the good ship Venus, Bless 'em all (adjusted version), *The Ball of Kirriemuir* and many more. Someone nudged my elbow and nodding towards Tom said, 'He's on the gin and lemons, we'll be getting *Eskimo Nell*'. After about three triple gins on top of numerous pints of beer, Tom stood at the fireplace in the Officers' Mess and recited the whole of that epic narrative poem known as *Eskimo Nell.* It was the first time that I had heard the complete work and I was astonished at the complexity of the piece and the feat of memory that could bring it so alive before us. He just about managed to acknowledge our applause before passing out.

We chatted with many people including Wing Commander John Molesworth, his once ginger handlebar moustache now snow white, and Willie Whitehouse the gunnery leader. Willie, when he was on ops, seemed to attract German fighters like flies but he always saw them first, which is why he survived the war with a double DFC.

Harry Rich, the Flight Engineer of the crew with which I did my first operation, informed me that his Skipper, F/Lt Winder, had been killed in a road accident some years ago. When I kidded him about the non welcome I got from his crew before the raid on Frankfurt, he replied, 'Oh we were a pretty superstitious bunch – you were our first 'second dickey' and we were all shit scared'.

Many other faces were familiar but the time came to attend the service before we had a chance to speak to them, or have lunch.

The band from RAF Cranwell in full dress uniform provided the music. RAF Swinderby provided the guard of honour at the memorial and the 12 Squadron colour with full escort was paraded. RAF Newton provided a team to record the ceremony on videotape and Bishop Cocks, former Chaplain in Chief to the RAF, conducted the service.

At 3.40pm precisely, the last flying Lancaster of the RAF, 'City of Lincoln', roared over the memorial in salute to our fallen comrades. The Lanc flew four passes, the last one being below roof top height. It was a fitting culmination to a very memorable and moving occasion and one which those of us who were present will never forget.

After the service we returned to the White Hart where the landlord and his staff were serving very welcome teas. Tubby and I decided to attend next year's reunion dinner and to get in touch with the rest of the crew. That night Tubby had a party at his house when I met his wife, son and two daughters and their friends.

* * * * *

On Monday morning I set off North. Tubby had given me Don Leader's last known address in Darlington and I had confidently said, 'If he's alive, I'll find him'.

The trail took me to Darlington, to Sedgefield, to Morton-on-Swale near Northallerton, then to Scotch Corner.

His neighbours in the quiet village of Morton-on-Swale had informed me that he was warden of the caravan site at Scotch Corner. Seemingly it was only a temporary post to help out a friend. Don would be over 70 years old now.

As I approached the entrance gate of the site, I recognised Don who was looking through the window of the warden's luxury caravan. Going up to the window, I put out my tongue at him. As I had recognised him, I fully expected him to recognise me, but of course I was looking for him whereas he was not expecting to suddenly see me after 37 years. Thinking I was a cheeky representative of some firm or other, he imperiously waved me round to the door. Ella his wife, who I had never met, let me in. I said, 'It's that old 'B' I want to see, I'll see you later'. Scowling, as only Don could, he said, 'I don't know what you are selling but I don't want any'.

From that inauspicious start and eventual recognition, this turned out to be a marvellous reunion. I heard Ella on the telephone to their daughter Pat in Richmond, 'Your Dad's pilot from the war has turned up, you and Alan must come along'.

Don's friends owned the 'Vintage' restaurant and bar along with the caravan site. That evening after a superb meal we chatted and reminisced until midnight. I was put up in the spare room in the caravan.

We discovered, amazingly, that we were both stationed at No. 16 Ferry Unit, St Mawgan in Cornwall, in the summer of 1946 before we were both demobbed. I was there with a Transport Command crew waiting to ferry Halifaxes to the French Atlantic Weather Flight and Don, now a Warrant Officer, was in charge of the Station Transport unit. If only we had known.

After demob Don went back to engineering with a firm who designed weaving machines and was transferred to ICI. He retired early with an injured back but this did not stop him from pursuing his great liking for motor caravaning, travelling all over Britain.

Before taking my leave next day, Don had telephoned Tubby and arranged a meeting with him somewhere midway between Lincoln and Scotch Corner.

Some weeks later I heard sad news from Tubby. He had put in a request to a Sheffield – 'Where are you now?' radio programme giving the necessary details of Frank Fathers and requesting that he get in touch. One of Frank's sons had heard the broadcast and got his mother to phone Tubby informing him that Frank had died three years ago. She said he had been a loving husband and father to their two sons.

Early the following year, I was in the local library perusing a technical book – *Grinding Lapping & Honing*, when to my surprise at the end of the book I came across the following:

'The illustrations of honing equipment in this book are reproduced by courtesy of Messrs. Gaston E. Marbaix, Ltd.'

The main factory and head office was in Basingstoke, so I phoned there and was put through to his private secretary. She said that Mr Marbaix was abroad on a business trip and would not be back until the following Monday. I told her that I was a wartime friend of someone called Gus Marbaix and asked if he might possibly have been stationed at Wickenby during the war. She said that she was sure that he had served with Bomber Command so I explained the purpose of my call and left my name and telephone number.

On Monday morning the telephone rang, 'Hello Jock, I just got your message – how wonderful, I never knew if you had got 'the chop' or not after I left the crew'. We chatted for a long time. He said that he would most certainly make the reunion at the Holiday Inn, Leicester, in September, but would like to meet Don, Tubby and I before that if possible.

Then in June, out of the blue, I received a letter from Stan Moore which had been posted in America. Stan and his wife Pat were on a three-month world tour and would be arriving in a London hotel in two weeks time. He asked me if I would I write to him there and arrange a meeting. My letter giving full details was waiting for him when he checked in.

Our first meeting was in an Edinburgh Hotel. I recognised him immediately, a bit thin on top but the same old Stan. My wife Barbara and Stan's wife Pat listened most tolerantly as we flew again in the wartime skies over Germany.

Life had been good to Stan after the war. Getting his licence as a State bookmaker he was able to follow his favourite sports – horse racing and sulkey trotting – and to make a good living in the process.With two sons and four daughters and an increasing number of grandchildren, Stan and Pat were very contented and were enjoying their extended holiday.

He told me that as soon as he had read my letter, he had dashed off a letter to Greg Mayes in Sydney in the hope that he might just be able to fly over for the reunion in Leicester. Stan had met Greg four or five times since the war and thought he was doing very well in the Insurance business. Greg's hobby was sailing and he owned a fair size yacht. As far as Stan knew Greg had only one son, Nigel.

In August I received a long letter from Greg in which he stated that he would do his damnedest to get to the reunion in September. The next I would hear would be him telephoning details of his flight into London airport.

In the interim, Stan and Pat had managed to meet Gus, Tubby and Don at a rendezvous in their respective localities. They also managed to stay with us in Dundee from where we travelled to Aberdeen to meet up with my son and renew contact with wartime friends.

Don had insisted that Barbara and I stay overnight with them in Moreton-on-Swale on the Friday before the reunion and then travel together to Leicester the next day, 25 September for the reunion dinner and dance in the

Holiday Inn. He had also arranged a rendezvous with Tubby and his wife Jean so that we would all arrive at Leicester together.

Greg phoned me on the Thursday and informed me that the only flight he could get would be via Holland and that he would not get to London until Sunday forenoon. I said that I would meet him at Heathrow and take him to Wickenby for the memorial service.

On Saturday lunchtime I pulled my nondescript vehicle into a parking space next to that occupied by a gleaming Rolls-Royce. This it turned out belonged to Gus and his wife Mary who had just arrived having also brought Stan and Pat with them. Then Tubby and Jean pulled in and we were ages chatting in the car park before going into the hotel.

Although I recognised Gus immediately on setting eyes on him, he seemed taller and more debonair now. When he first joined our crew he had not been long married to Mary, a serving WAAF, and they were living out in Lincoln whenever he got the opportunity. Consequently I did not see much of him socially. Mary, laughing, said, 'I'm sorry Jock that our first meeting way back in February 1945 was not really a pleasant one'. Then I remembered that, when Gus was informed by Wing Commander Molesworth that he was tour expired, I had asked him if he wanted to carry on with us. Gus said that he was willing to do so but that I would have to meet his wife and get her permission first. That night we met at the Saracen's Head in Lincoln. Mary must have known that the purpose of the introduction was not entirely a social one and while Gus was at the bar getting a round of drinks, and before I had even broached the subject, she said, 'Don't ask, the answer would be a definite no'. That was the last time I had seen them until now, a gap of nearly 38 years.

We finally got into the bar and were all chatting away furiously until little time was left to check into our rooms and get ready for the big do that evening.

Assembling again at 7pm in the bar, we were certainly a happy lot as we moved into the dining hall. Then we learned that this was Don and Ella's wedding anniversary so Stan started the ball rolling and ordered three bottles of champagne. It was so difficult for us to keep silent during the toasts and speeches.

It was after 2am when we all retired to our rooms. Stan had volunteered to come with me to pick up Greg from Heathrow even though I would have to set off at 7am without any breakfast. As I got to my car, spot on seven, good old dependable Stan was there.

The plane arrived on time. As we watched the passengers troop through the gates we both shouted simultaneously, 'That's him' even though Greg was sporting a bushy beard and moustache. It showed that when you live and fly with someone day and night for a whole year, their characteristics give them away.

On the long run up to Wickenby we recalled the operations. It was clear to me that, even in the same aircraft, each crew member had retained a different perspective of an operation, which was obvious when you think about it. A bomb-aimer lying in the nose sees much more of what goes on underneath than any other member of the crew. The wireless operator, apart from popping up to look out of the astrodome now and then, sees little more than the navigator who is behind the blackout curtain. The gunners are seeing more or less where we have been. The engineer is too preoccupied with his gauges and keeping up his log sheet to look out much. The pilot has a wide expansive view from the big perspex cockpit of a Lancaster, and would be looking out all the time, unless in cloud.

We arrived at Wickenby 20 minutes before the service was due to start. Greg received a great welcome from Don, Gus, Tubby and the wives. Photographs were taken of the six of us on this historic occasion.

Assembling at the memorial at 3pm, a guard of honour from RAF Swinderby, the Station Commander and the Civic Dignitaries of Lincoln were all in position when the skies opened with a monsoon type deluge. Everyone got drenched before making for the shelter of cars and coaches. After about 30 minutes the skies cleared and with typical Wickenby fortitude we went on with the service. Unfortunately, however, the break down in the weather prevented the 'City of Lincoln' Lancaster from doing its fly past.

That evening Tubby had arranged with the owner of the Floral Hotel in Caistor for a meal to be laid on. When we arrived there was a lovely fire going in the old style dining room, which was much appreciated by all of us, especially the Australians. Greg had a bottle of Crawfords five star from the 'duty free' and we were soon in high spirits again.

Afterwards we all went to Tubby's local pub in Caistor, which we took over. Tubby was in great form and one of the stories, which he related, I had completely forgotten. That was the time we had been diverted to the American airfield at Framlingham and the Yanks dished out as much whisky as we wanted as long as they got a signature for each large measure. Tubby went on, 'Greg got writer's cramp and the Skipper, being an Aberdonian, matched him glass for glass'. I remembered that bit all right but Tubby carried on, 'Next day, Frank and I heard the Lancs starting up so we made our way to the dispersal. Imagine our surprise when Roger 2 passed us on the peri track. We were shouting and waving but it carried on and took off without us. We had to thumb a lift from one of the other Lancs. I said to Frank at the time that the Skipper must still be half pissed from all that free whisky'.

When Tubby mentioned Frank, I detected the sadness in the others that he was not with us on this otherwise happy occasion. We had shared a common experience, an experience shared by relatively few of our contemporaries; an experience of such awesome proportions that only those who had gone through the same or similar could appreciate its enormity.

But it was this experience which enabled us to assess each other's worth. Only we know what the others had to face and through this knowledge we built up our mutual affection and respect.

The stories and laughter carried on way past closing time when we all went back to Tubby's house where we partook of strong coffee and sandwiches.

Eventually we had to say farewell. I remember big Stan had tears in his eyes – did he sense then that we would never see each other again? Then Gus, Mary, Stan, Pat and Greg drove south, while Don, Ella, Barbara and I headed north.

Chapter 21
EPILOGUE

I tried my best to keep in touch with the others after we parted at Tubby's house and Barbara and I went on several holidays with Don and Ella. However, as I write this almost 30 years later, Don, Stan, Tubby and Gus have all since passed on and therefore Greg in Australia and myself are now the only ones still around.

Of those no longer with us Gus was the most recent to go and after learning of his death I submitted an article in tribute to his memory which was published in the Spring 2009 issue of the *Wickenby Register Newsletter* entitled – 'Memories of Gus (Gaston) Marbaix'.

He was awarded the DFC like myself and I mentioned in chapter 18 that I had learned of my award in April 1945 after I finished my tour of operations. The DFC was granted only to officers and warrant officers (Gus as a navigator had the rank of Flying Officer) to recognise acts of 'valour, courage or devotion to duty performed while flying in active operations against the enemy'. Such medals were normally presented to recipients at a ceremony by the King in person. However, mine arrived in the post at my home in Aberdeen with a letter signed by King George VI explaining that unfortunately he was not well enough to attend a medals ceremony at the time.

After receiving my medal I never took the trouble to investigate what the recommendations which led to the award may have said. It wasn't until I had got in touch with Gus again after all those years that he managed to obtain copies of both our recommendations which included the terms of the initial recommendation by our Squadron Commander followed by the remarks of the Station and Base Commanders and finally those of the then No. 1 Group Commander AVM R.S. Blucke. Modesty forbids me from describing the terms of my own recommendation in any detail other than to say that it made reference in general to the various targets we attacked and more specifically to the raid on Essen on 23 October 1944 when we lost half of our starboard wing. The recommendations for Gus, however, who completed a total of 42 sorties spanning two tours, paid tribute *inter alia* to his high standard of skill and initiative as a navigator and that his best use of the aids at his disposal had contributed in no small measure to the fine record of his captain and crew.

The other five crew members were all NCOs and accordingly were not eligible for the award of a DFC. However, they were instead potentially eligible for the award of a DFM (Distinguished Flying Medal) which carried exactly the same criteria of valour, courage etc. as for the DFC. The fact that none of them did get this honour is not surprising when I tell you that the DFM accounted for less than a quarter of the combined total of DFCs and DFMs awarded during World War Two. This seems incomprehensible to me when you consider that more than 70 per cent of Bomber Command aircrew were NCOs. I hope I have made it abundantly clear by now in this book that in my view the rest of our crew were as equally deserving as Gus and I of any awards that might be going.

For my own part, after the disbandment of 612 in 1957, I carried on working as a janitor at Ruthrieston School where we occupied the 'jannies lodge' there on Holburn Street. Jim Healy, who had a wallpaper shop on George Street, and I were also fortunate to obtain weekend employment as radar operators at RAF Buchan near Peterhead on a Flight Lieutenant's pay which was good money. Those were still the years of the 'Cold War' and part of our job involved tracking the Russian 'Bears' which were a type of long range Tupalev bomber and signalling to RAF Leuchars to send jets to intercept and shadow them. This all apparently became a bit of a game with our airmen waving to the Soviet crews and vice versa. However, there was, of course, a deadly serious undercurrent to all this activity and how Jim and I wished we were up there flying the now state of the art RAF jets instead of being stuck in the radar control room. However, we both knew sadly that our time as pilots was now irrevocably over.

The part-time work at RAF Buchan lasted until 1961 but in those four years I still somehow found time away from that and the full-time job to indulge in a few sidelines including breeding budgerigars and a short-lived spell as a bookie in partnership with two pals at the dog track near the Old Bridge of Dee, the site of which is now occupied by an Asda superstore. A succession of short priced favourites romping home in the handful of meetings we attended exhausted our capital and put a premature end to that venture. We had a few laughs while it lasted though.

After the job at RAF Buchan ended I decided to leave the 'janitorial profession' and we moved from the lodge at Ruthrieston to nearby Gairn Terrace. Over the next decade or so I mainly worked as a travelling sales rep trying to persuade people to place an order for everything from welding equipment to even mobile cranes at one point.

Thereafter once my first marriage ended around 1970, I moved not long afterwards to Dundee where I married Barbara and worked latterly as a hospital engineer for Tayside Health Board until my retirement in 1987. Barbara passed away some years ago but I remain very close to some of her relatives and I still live in Dundee with my two cats for company. The passing years have inevitably taken their toll on my former colleagues in 612. Of my own inner circle of friends from those days only Bill Innes and the irrepressible Jim Healy – with whom I still keep in touch and who must have outlived even some of his jokes by now! – are still around.

Looking back on a long and largely happy life I can't help but reflect how fortunate my fellow crew members and I were to come through the war unscathed. The odds were significantly against us given the number of operations we flew and I can readily recall several occasions when we almost 'bought it' – we were indeed the lucky ones.

I referred in chapter 18 to the lack of official recognition over many years for those who died flying for Bomber Command and the hurt this must have caused their relatives. I was therefore gratified to learn that, following a lengthy campaign, a fitting memorial to honour the 55,573 men of Bomber Command who lost their lives in World War Two is currently under construction in London's Green Park and is expected to be unveiled by Her Majesty the Queen at a ceremony in June 2012. For those of us who survived and are still here, this will go a long way to rectifying a major injustice and means a great deal.

BIBLIOGRAPHY

Bishop, Patrick *Bomber Boys* (Harper Press, 2007)

Currie, Jack *Lancaster Target* (Goodall Publications, 1981)

Falconer, Jonathan *Bomber Command Handbook* (Sutton Publishing, 1998)

Franks, Norman *Ton-Up Lancs* (Grub Street, 2005)

Hastings, Max *Bomber Command* (Michael Joseph, 1979)

Middlebrook, Martin *The Nuremberg Raid* (Penguin Books, 1973)

Middlebrook, Martin and Everitt, Chris *The Bomber Command War Diaries* (Midland Publishing, 1985)

Nicholl, John and Rennell, Tony *Tail-End Charlies* (Penguin Books, 2004)

McKinstry, Leo *Lancaster* (John Murray, 2009)

Taylor, Frederick *Dresden* (Bloomsbury, 2004)

Tripp, Miles *The Eighth Passenger* (Wordsworth Editions, 1969)

Yates, Harry *Luck and a Lancaster* (Airlife Publishing, 1999)

INDEX

Abbey Lodge Medical Centre, London 23
Air Crew Receiving Centre, Lords Cricket Ground, London 22–23, 26
Alexander Hall & Co., Shipbuilders, Aberdeen 11
Anson aircraft 39
Auchinleck, General Claude 28
Auxiliary Airforce – 612 (County of Aberdeen) Squadron, 8, 165–66, 168, 170–71, 185–86

Baker, W/Cdr 'Tubby' 117
Balford, F/Lt Bill 70
Balzer, Rudi 5, 70–72
Bawtry Hall, nr Doncaster, Yorks 84–85
Bennet, F/O R.C. 139–40
Berlin, 'battle of' 69
Bisset, Captain 42
Blucke, AVM R.S. 185
Bochum, bombing raid 158
Bolderston, F/Lt G.T. 55–56, 62–63, 69
Bomber Command
  1 Group 6, 54, 55, 68, 83, 84, 99, 115, 150, 156, 157, 185
  3 Group 58
  4 Group 117, 129
  5 Group 84, 115, 122
  6 Group 132
  12 Squadron 55, 56, 70, 129, 151, 156, 177
  100 Squadron 92
  153 Squadron 118
  626 Squadron 7, 55, 56, 62, 69, 70, 103, 106, 139, 140, 149, 156, 158, 175
  Bircotes, Notts – Operational Training Unit 47, 112
  Blyton, Lincs – Heavy Conversion Unit 51–52, 146
  Finningley, Yorks – OTU 47, 51
  Hemswell, Lincs – No.1 Lancaster Finishing School 52, 55
  Lindholme, Yorks – OTU 45–46
  Little Rissington, Oxon – Pilots Advanced Flying Unit 45
  Swinderby, Lincs – HCU 159–60, 177, 182
  Wickenby Airfield, Lincs (12 & 626 Squadrons) 115, 117, 125, 128–29, 140, 147–48, 155–57, 159, 175–76, 179, 182
Boutwood, Captain John 43
Bradwell Bay, Essex 95
Bursey, F/O C.M. 140

Caledonian Hotel, Aberdeen 97, 125
Campbell, F/O 76, 78
Catalina Flying Boat 38, 77
Charland, F/O 76, 78
Charlottetown, Prince Edward Island, Canada 31
Charter Hall Training Station, Scottish Borders 106, 125
Chemnitz, bombing raid 124, 130, 134, 140, 161
Cherry, F/Lt Len 165

Cheshire, AVM John 173
Child, S/Ldr Joe 50, 166
Churchill, Sir Winston 13
Clayton, F/Sgt Arthur 47, 51, 82, 91, 101–02, 112, 114, 118, 122, 128, 133, 135, 140, 147, 152, 154–55, 159, 175–76, 178–84
Collens, F/O 62
Cologne, bombing raids 86, 120, 128–29, 137, 141, 160
Cooper, Andy 171
Cory, S/Ldr Guy 171
Cox, F/Lt L.J. 156
Crerar, Air Commodore Finlay 173
Croswell, Corporal 24
Cummins, Gordon ('The Blackout Ripper') 8, 25–26
Curacao, HMS 43–44

Dalgleish, F/Lt Jock 165–66
De Salis, F/Lt Tim 171
De Wesselow, S/Ldr C.P.C. 122
Dilley, Alex 19
Dimbleby, Sir Richard 118–19
Dinard, Brittany, France 166
Dobson, F/Lt 49
Dortmund, bombing raids 90, 125, 143, 160
Dresden, bombing raid 10, 84, 120–23, 135, 160–61
Driver, F/O 159
Duisburg, bombing raid 49, 74, 76, 78, 125, 160
Dusseldorf, bombing raid 86, 101, 160
Dyce Airfield, Aberdeen 12, 50, 165–66, 168, 170–74

Eames, F/lt 159
Emmerich, bombing raid 68–69
Enciso-y-Sieglie, F/O Moje 138
Essen, bombing raids 80–81, 83, 85–86, 100, 103, 138, 104–43, 147, 158, 160, 185

Fanner, P/O Bill 130, 133–34, 140
Fathers, F/Sgt Frank 47, 111, 159, 179
Fisk, F/O 152
Foy, F/O 157
Forsyth Hotel, Aberdeen 19–20
Frankfurt am Main, bombing raid 57, 61–63, 78, 109–10, 120, 122, 133, 157, 177
Framlingham, Suffolk – USAAF base 88–89
Franks, Norman 139
Freiburg, bombing raid 90

Garland, Victor 21
Gee, F/Lt John 119
German fighter aircraft
  Focke Wulf 190 91, 102, 138, 147
  Junkers 88 91
  Messerschmitt 109 91, 147
  ME 110 70, 91
  ME 262 90
German fighter tactics
  Wilde Sau 91
  Zahme Sau 91
  Von unter hinten 92
  Schrage Musik 92–94, 111, 156
Gemmer, Hans 71
Gibson, F/Lt 38
Good, F/O Al 127, 157
Gordon, Harold 20
Gordon, F/Lt Sandy 50, 165
Gray, F/Lt Peter 170
Greeno, Detective Inspector 25–26
Grindrod, F/Lt 115
Grosse Ile, Michigan, USA – training base 34–35

Halfaya Pass, Egypt 27
Halifax 5 bomber 51, 54
Halifax 7 transport 164
Halifax, Nova Scotia 41
Hall Russell, Shipbuilders, Aberdeen 11–14
Hanau, bombing raid 157
Harris, Sir Arthur 73, 136, 144
Harrogate, Yorks 44–45
Harvard trainer aircraft 38, 165–66
Hawarden, Cheshire 168
Haynes, G/Cpt 61
Healy, F/Lt Jim 165, 172, 185–86
Heaton Park, Manchester – Aircrew Holding Unit 31–32
Heimbach, bombing raid 90
Holiday Inn, Leicester 180
Holloway, F/O 125
Horrocks, Lt/Gen Brian 118
Hutcheon, George 167, 173

Illingworth, Captain Gordon 44
Imlah, Herbert 167